Divinely Aligned

Divinely Aligned
Poetry

Rachel Heaney

Portal Of Bliss

Copyright © 2023 by Rachel Heaney

All rights reserved. No part of this book may be reproduced in any manner whatsoever without written permission except in the case of brief quotations embodied in critical articles and reviews.

First Printing, 2023

Contents

1 Miracles Of Life 1

2 Service & Support 2

3 Committed To Grow 3

4 Which Way To Go 4

5 Sailing South 5

6 Fitzroy Island 6

7 Poetic Healing 7

8 Hinchinbrook Mystery 8

9 Island Of Density 9

10 Fashion Transcends 10

11 Mirror Of Truth 11

12 Integrity Is The Key 12

13 The Phoenix 13

14 Breaking Old Patterns 14

15 Foreign Feeling 15

Contents

16 Dark Night Of The Soul 16

17 Divine Messages 17

18 Freeing Past Pains 18

19 Taught To Be Tough 19

20 Stuck 20

21 Sleep Deprived 21

22 The Space Between 22

23 Web Of Creativity 23

24 Artificial Division 24

25 Collective Rebirth 25

26 The Irony 26

27 Gateway Of Grief 27

28 A Time Of Giving Presence 28

29 Christmas Day 29

30 Christmas Spirit 30

31 Seeds Of Attachment 31

32 Creating A Dream 33

33 What Would Love Do 34

34 Self-Motivation 35

Contents

35   Energy Speaks   36

36   Deeper Trust   37

37   Rewards Of Letting Go   38

38   Intuition Makes No Sense   39

39   Lured In   40

40   Ultimate Duality   41

41   Not Open To Receive   42

42   What Is Real   43

43   Energy Of The Tree   44

44   That Off Feeling   45

45   In The Silence   46

46   In Full Flow Effect   47

47   Heart Expansion   48

48   Honour Self   49

49   Authentic Leadership   50

50   Magic Moments   51

51   Highest Good Of All   52

52   Letting Go Of The Grip   53

53   Divine Plan   54

Contents

54   This Moment   55

55   Inner Union   56

56   Void Of Change   57

57   Worthy Of Love   58

58   Redirection   59

59   Speak Your Truth   60

60   Purpose   61

61   Don't Ignore The Call   62

62   Let Love In   64

63   Glimpse In Their Eyes   65

64   Abundance Is Energy   66

65   Give & Receive In Full Flow   68

66   Blooming Of The Rose   70

67   Conscious Awareness   71

68   Rainbow Bridge   72

69   Physical Upgrade   74

70   Wishes   75

71   Soul Journey   76

72   Beyond The Body   77

Contents

73 You Hold The Key 78

74 Journey Of Self-Acceptance 79

75 Love As My Guide 80

76 Mind Battle 82

77 Desire To Be Met 83

78 So Simple 84

79 It's Already Yours 85

80 Effortless Flow 86

81 Existence 87

82 Life Responds To Vibration 88

83 Be Happy 89

84 Momentum Of Flow 90

85 Simply Live 91

86 Divinity Of Flow 92

87 Your Guide Through Life 93

88 Sun Lover 94

89 Momentum Of Flowing 95

90 Internal Validation 96

91 Secret To Life 97

Contents

92   Attraction Or Distraction   98

93   Chi Chats   99

94   Monkey In Your Mind   100

95   Freedom For The Brave   101

96   Packing Up   102

97   Divine Unfolding   103

98   Reflection Of You   104

99   Sweet Spot Within   105

100   Expectation & Boundaries   106

101   Daily Alignment   107

102   Flames   109

103   Tuned In   110

104   The Calling Of This Book   111

105   Honour The Truth Inside   112

106   Change Your Thoughts   113

107   Seeking   114

108   Exploring   115

109   Clarity   116

110   Back To Your Heart   117

Contents

111   Divinely Aligned   118

112   Humble Men   119

113   Dream Spell   120

114   Remembering The Love   121

115   Unification   122

116   Polarity   123

117   Heart Based Reality   124

118   Peace On Earth   125

119   Rhythmic Life   126

120   Harmonize   127

121   The Innocent Gift   128

122   Disconnect To Reconnect   129

123   Your Own Whispers   131

124   Dedicated To Be   132

125   A True Gift   133

126   Divinely Aligned Mirror   134

127   Social Anxiety   135

128   The Truth You Will Find   136

129   Nurtured By He   137

Contents

130   The Key To All You Crave   138

131   Gifts Of Life   139

132   The Compass Inside Of You   140

133   Out-Dated Beliefs   141

134   Outside The Box   142

135   Have The Courage   143

136   Your Internal Map   144

137   The Program, Programming You   145

138   Labels & Identities   146

139   The Earth's Crystal Core   147

140   Free Will   148

141   Stillness & Art   150

142   Offering Of Gratitude   151

143   Out Of The Blue   152

144   Here To Create   153

145   Animal Guidance   154

146   Principles & Guides   155

147   Magical Orchestration   156

148   The Gift Of Rain   157

Contents

149   Self-Generate Energy   158

150   Divine Man   159

151   The Truth   160

152   Peace That Resides In You   161

153   Seeds Of Truth   162

154   The Pain Body   163

155   Life Force   164

156   Godly Self   165

157   Truth Whispers   166

158   Love Of Life   167

159   A Divine Reflection   168

160   Bio Field Activation   170

161   Transcending The Mind   171

162   Feeling Content Within   172

163   Concrete Jungle   173

164   New Level Of Shielding Needed   174

165   Contraction & Expansion   175

166   Karma Clearing   176

167   Synchronistic Feeling   177

Contents

168 New Level Of Sensitivity 178

169 Road Trip Back To Oneness 179

170 Pleasure Of Simplicity 181

171 Floating Beauty 182

172 The Most Rewarding Gift 183

173 Ocean Of Love 184

174 Heightened Senses 185

175 She Is Nature 186

176 Heavenly Existence 187

177 Natural High 188

178 Loving Creativity 189

179 Birth & Being 190

180 Those That Align 191

181 Sacred Heart 192

182 Weeding The Old 193

183 Rainforest Bliss 194

184 Who Am I 195

185 To Give Is The Gift 196

186 Back To The Core 197

Contents

187 Secret To Living 198

188 Peace In The Heart 199

189 Waking Up To The Illusion 200

190 Stop And Be 201

191 Water The Flowers 202

192 Taking Flight 203

193 Demons Of The Mind 204

194 Compassion Lives In The Heart 205

195 Greed And Wealth 206

196 Question Within 208

197 Releasing Addiction 209

198 Vibration Is A Choice 210

199 Present Gift 211

200 Sea Change 212

201 Planting The Seeds 213

202 Treasure Map 214

203 Connect To The Heart 215

204 Presence Of Love 216

205 What Are You Creating 217

Contents

206 Divinely Aligned Timing 218

207 Switch Off 219

208 The First Breath 220

209 Prioritise Rest 222

210 How To Handle Grief 223

211 Dream Meaning 224

212 Confusion 225

213 Healing Journey 226

214 Waking Up to A New Day 227

215 Love, In Full Flow 229

216 Blessings From Above 230

217 Down To Earth 231

218 Decluttering The Mind 232

219 Christmas In the Eyes of a Child 233

220 Love Is Our Savior 235

221 State Of Lust 236

222 Sliding Door Moments 237

223 False Light 239

224 Twists & Turns 240

Contents

Acknowledgement **241**

{ 1 }

Miracles Of Life

I'd announced it the day before,
Sailing amongst islands, is what I adore...
I was calling in a sailing trip,
And wow, it happened so quick...
The next day I got offered some mermaid time,
On the water, in the sun, is where I truly shine...
There was not too much time to think it through,
I just knew what it was I had to do...
Say 'yes' to this magical trip of a lifetime,
It was a beautiful gift from the divine...
Because I'd followed through on my poetry book,
I'd been rewarded for all the dedication it took...
This is also something I teach others to do,
To be open to the miracles of life as they reward you...

{ 2 }

Service & Support

Continue to commit to yourself,
So you can be of service to everyone else...
Each day call upon your inner being,
To show you the next step in creating your dream...
Helping you to take action each day,
By listening to what the guidance has to say...
Finding many creative ways to be of service,
You not taking action, is a disservice...
Everything you've been through has paved the way,
So you can support others, and feel lit up each day...

Committed To Grow

If you're committed to grow, and lead the way,
You listen to what your guidance has to say...
You say 'yes' when it's a full body yes,
Because you don't want to live life with regrets...
The mind may come in to bring you fear,
But the only way that fear will disappear...
Is if you have that deep trust in yourself,
And don't take on the fears of everyone else...
Just take that leap into the unknown,
All your pathways will be shown...
A shift will occur with that leap,
And so many benefits you will reap...
It can seem scary, I've been here plenty of times before,
And I know there is so much expansion and so much more...

{ 4 }

Which Way To Go

Sometimes life has a plan that we may not know,
There will be decisions to make on which way to go...
They all lead to the same destination,
So you must decide without hesitation...
When it's a full body yes it comes before the mind,
Within the full body goosebumps, are the answers I find...
So I say 'yes' before the mind gets in the way,
Blocking out the fears, and doubt it has to say...
Because when I trust in me,
It allows me to feel so free...
And I know I'm here to help others too,
By being the embodiment of living so true...

Sailing South

The sight of sunlight shimmering on the ocean,
Is what sets my inner sails in full motion...
Looking out the window of the plane,
I see all the islands that still remain...
Beauty everywhere the eyes could see,
I could feel the bliss inside of me...
There is something about islands that lights me up,
One of the ways that really fills my cup...
Being on a boat sailing the sea,
Is what has me feeling so free...
Tomorrow, we head out sailing south,
Constant awe, as my jaw drops from my mouth...
Dolphins, whales and turtles to see,
And lots of learning to sail for me...

Fitzroy Island

Sailing to a new island I have never been,
So spacious, beautiful and so serene...
Secret garden walking trails,
Being in nature never fails...
It takes us back to our peace within,
Where nature and humanity both win...
Sunsets overlooking the water and mainland,
A beauty many wouldn't understand...
Because they may not take time to be,
Or know what it's like to feel so free...
It's a simple life on the ocean,
The wind and waves keeping you in motion...
There is no place I'd rather be,
Than when I have the ocean surrounding me...
Where is a place that makes you feel alive,
Maybe it's under the water you like to dive...
There's another world down there waiting for you to explore,
A place where you will realise, you need no more...

Poetic Healing

A couple of years ago, I was heading to Airlie Beach,
Not knowing it was a new level of love, I would reach...
Not a love for somebody else,
I was embodying loving myself...
There were so many challenges I had to face,
And Airlie was the perfect place...
I felt abandoned by those I love,
But I trusted in the guidance from above...
It was an initiation I had to go through,
Which I knew before I truly knew...
Poetry was how I processed all that was going on,
And it was showing me where I do belong...
There was another layer opened into my heart,
And it helped birth my poetry art...
The book that I birthed is called 'In Full Flow',
I'm so grateful I trusted where I was guided to go...

Hinchinbrook Mystery

There was something incredible about this land,
Mountains so tall I couldn't understand...
How have I not heard about this place,
The energy coming from this sacred space...
I was in awe like never before,
It gave me a transmission and so much more...
Standing almost 1000 meters tall,
It was the most beautiful nature wall...
I felt the energy coming through,
And insights I never knew...
I felt the spirits living underground,
Their frequency I had just found...
I wondered how long they had been here for,
And if they got many visitors come to shore...
It took a while for us to sail along,
And there was a familiarity of where I'm from...

Island Of Density

There was something that didn't feel quite right,
From the moment it entered my sight...
The energy was dense & felt so rough,
Purging the energy was still not enough...
I didn't sleep so great anchored there,
Noises through the night that were so rare...
I feared someone was going to come onboard,
Maybe we had things they couldn't afford...
There were also planes flying low in the night,
To me, that doesn't feel quite right...
What is that island actually about,
More than we are taught to believe, I have no doubt...
The news said it's 'the worst place on Earth',
I feel they are hiding something, for what it's worth...

Fashion Transcends

What even is fashion, I sometimes ask,
Following someone's rules, is that the task...
But who is it, that makes the rules,
Are the people who follow, the real fools...
I've never been one to follow the pack,
Because I feel it sometimes comes from a place of lack...
Sure, follow the fashion if you like what you see,
Or wear what you want, to truly feel free...
Know that your unique style is your own fashion brand,
Sit with that for a minute, and let it land...
What do you feel your best dressed in,
Maybe that is where your fashion trend will begin...
Let go of the rules of what you think you have to do,
And just be fully, authentically you...

Mirror Of Truth

It's a strange thing to sometimes receive,
All the words that we don't want to believe...
But when we slowly allow them in,
We feel our heart start to sing...
This may be a foreign feeling that you've never felt,
So can you open to this gift you've been dealt...
That thing you've yearned for, for so long,
In your heart is where it may belong...
Or maybe it's been there the entire time,
You just haven't met your mirror to the divine...
Sometimes the mirrors may not be very clear,
There may be fogginess or some sort of smear...
But when that mirror shows up shining,
You deep down know that it's divine timing...
Because you won't see a clear reflection from anyone else,
If you haven't yet committed to yourself...
So how can you clear your own mirror face,
In divine timing, it is not a race...

Integrity Is The Key

Integrity is the base for your existence,
So is it an area you have resistance...
Do you stay true to what you say you'll do,
If not, life will reflect it back to you...
For so long I wouldn't follow through on things for myself,
I'd abandon me, to support everyone else...
Wondering why I never felt met back,
Showing how much I'd fallen off track...
You see, life is a mirror of our internal state,
So you must start within, with what you want to create...
Because if life presents something you don't want to see,
Doing the inner work is the ultimate key...
It will unlock all the patterns at play,
And you'll see it reflected back in your day...
Your life can change for the better ultra-quick,
Being integral to yourself is the trick...
So give it a try and you will be shown,
How many old patterns you have outgrown...
Life will reward you in the most beautiful way,
Because the mirror of life reflects back each day...

The Phoenix

The power of the phoenix rising,
Is a force of no describing...
It's an alchemical process of release,
So your light & frequency can increase...
It may feel overwhelming to some,
As there is so much to overcome...
The death of the old & birth of the new,
The phoenix rises from the ashes, it's true...
Maybe you may be in this process now,
If so, I invite you to trust somehow...
The phoenix symbolises fire & passion,
The catalyst to begin your soul mission...
It brings good luck, harmony, peace & prosperity,
And will eventually bring you so much clarity...

Breaking Old Patterns

As I drop into this feeling,
I see all that it's revealing...
I had to meet myself at the deepest level,
And forgive my ex, the so-called devil...
Because I now see how it was all part of the plan,
As I was calling in the most amazing man...
And for me to be able to align with him,
There was so much inner work I had to begin...
My ex showed me all the ways I didn't love myself,
And how I was seeking that love from someone else...
He treated me how I was treating me,
I was abandoning me, and the mirror helped me see...
The ways I wasn't safe to use my voice,
And how staying with him was my choice...
But why would I choose that for me,
Because deep down I didn't feel worthy...
So I was attracted to men that confirmed that belief,
Exiting out of that dynamic was the biggest relief...
It wasn't an easy task moving through all the pain,
But it's a path I had to walk so the pattern wouldn't remain...

Foreign Feeling

You know that exact thing you've been calling in,
That thing that just at the thought, would make your heart sing...
It may be something you've hoped for, for so long,
And wondered what you were doing that was so wrong...
Because it wasn't yet a part of your reality,
Was what you were calling in, union & duality...
If so, you would have kept being shown a mirror of you,
Showing a reflection of where doesn't feel true...
Until you found that union within yourself,
You are not going to find it from someone else...
So you commit to you, to heal these parts,
So you stop being attracted to closed hearts...
Then you align with another who is the mirror of the new you,
You feel connection, expansion & something that feels so true...
You realise you've attracted what you've always yearned for,
Your mind might create stories & so much more...
Making you feel unworthy & wanting to run away,
Because this is a foreign feeling when divine union is at play...
Having awareness as the ego tries to keep you safe,
There will be some edges you are needing to face...
Trusting the gift and allowing the walls to fall,
In the end, how far you lean in, is your call...

Dark Night Of The Soul

Have you ever felt like everything was falling away,
Wondering if life is worth it at the end of the day...
Please know that it is & you'll be out of the darkness soon,
And your life will then be in full bloom...
Like a seed that's planted into the Earth,
It may feel challenging through this rebirth...
In a dark place, waiting to breakthrough,
Where you'll then remember, what you forgot you knew...
A flower will open in divine timing,
Same as you, with all you are aligning...
Just know, there is no rushing through this part,
Nature doesn't rush, or force her beautiful art...
So please trust life is happening for you,
It may be hard to believe, but it is true...
Allow yourself to feel your growing pain,
Knowing soon this pain will no longer remain...
And you'll be shown in many beautiful ways,
You'll have gotten past this initiation phase...

{ 17 }

Divine Messages

Everything is connected, it's a universal law,
Once you remember that, you won't ignore...
The divine synchronicities that come your way,
Reminding you of the magic, every single day...
The gifts come to you when trusting this law,
You will no longer need for anything anymore...
Sometimes the plan is to have no plan,
To live life in flow, I am a huge fan...
It doesn't mean you will never fall off your track,
It just means your awareness will bring you back...
Reminding you how to be in alignment each day,
And trusting what the energy has to say...
People will appear out of the blue,
Bringing divine messages for you...
My question is, are you creating space in your day,
To listen to what your intuitive whispers have to say...
If the answer is no, take this as your sign,
If you start listening, the miracles will align...

Freeing Past Pains

May this book reach far & wide,
My poetry no longer wants to hide...
Many places across the planet, stocking my book,
People will be drawn to have a look...
They will find the way back to themselves,
And then ripple love back to everyone else...
The book acts as an awakening guide,
When we trust ourselves, we no longer have to hide...
We become magnetic to all we desire,
That is the energy that will also inspire...
It will inspire others who are walking the way,
We are all helping each other at the end of the day...
May this book reach the hands of those in need,
So of past patterns they can be freed...

Taught To Be Tough

I woke feeling sad for your inner little boy,
And how maybe he was forced into joy...
The times he had fallen and was broken,
The 'toughen up' words were spoken...
So he was taught to ignore the pain,
But that cellular pain would still remain...
Told to get up and go do the next thing,
Has left pressure hanging over him...
Always feeling he has to ignore his body's cues,
If it's broken bones or just a bruise...
It had taught him to be ultra-strong,
And maybe that feeling anything is wrong...
He was taught distraction from a young age,
To toughen up and be strong at every stage...
But maybe he needed a mother's gentle care,
So a woman's softness, for him, is ultra-rare...
And maybe that makes him want to run,
Before any union has even begun...

Stuck

Stuck in a job which no longer aligns,
I've been there before many times...
Each time knowing it's time to go,
Because I'm no longer in full flow...
But there is a part that fears to leave,
I know it's needed & is the key to receive...
Receive the gifts that will come my way,
When I honour me and walk away...
Because staying there means I abandon me,
And I want to live a life so free...
Free to trust what is true,
As miracles appear out of the blue...
So if you can relate then I want you to know,
Your soul mission is waiting for you to go...
So take that leap to release the pain,
You know in that job you aren't to remain...
So why torture yourself by staying in that job,
Because its your energy it will continue to rob...

Sleep Deprived

Sleep, without you I can't go on,
Lack of sleep feels so wrong...
I've taken you for granted, but not anymore,
Because it's you, I truly adore...
I feel myself yearning for you,
The strongest connection, it's true...
I hear you calling my name,
Wide awake, I don't want to remain...
Trying to push through each day,
With sleep, I also have energy to play...
Eight hours in your bliss is what I desire,
Because within me, there's so much you inspire...
Creativity comes through with such ease,
And I flow through the day, like a breeze...
But when I haven't been in your company enough,
It has me feeling drained, and so very rough...
I know I need to make more time for you,
So that's exactly what I'm going to do...

# The Space Between

The space between no words or thought,
Are the answers to all we haven't been taught…
That spaciousness between each breath out,
Before the next inhale comes about…
What in that moment wants to come through,
Is it a message sharing what is true…
Maybe it doesn't make sense to the mind,
Because beyond it, there is so much to find…
Allowing your spirit to journey through space,
Where time doesn't exist, & it isn't a race…
Collect the parts of you, you didn't know existed,
Not sure how, or why, you had resisted…
This space holds the key to all your desire,
And through stillness your DNA will rewire…
Allowing you to access many dimensions,
Releasing any human body tensions…
Then journal about where you went,
Where was it that you were sent…
And did you uncover more of your gifts,
As you realise your role as the consciousness shifts…

Web Of Creativity

The weaver of the web of creativity,
Is our own responsibility...
Creative energy can't be taught by another,
It's your own unique gift to discover...
And then share it in the ways you desire,
Which will act as a catalyst to inspire...
To inspire others to share their gift,
Because everyone has a unique essence which help uplift...
Raising the consciousness of the planet each day,
And also getting creative with lots of play...

Artificial Division

Another divide trying to take place,
Illuminating what we need to face...
Are we choosing love or fear,
Is there still judgement to clear...
Who is right or wrong,
Does this art not belong...
Or is it activating our past versions of ourselves,
Where we release projections from anyone else...
Allowing our expressions to come through in art,
Not allowing fear to remove us from our heart...
Everything in life has many points of view,
But do you allow one thought to consume you...
Or do you choose love over hate,
Maybe you just like a good debate...
My wish is for everyone is to trust their intuition,
Maybe also give themselves permission...
To do things that others may judge,
If we don't judge ourselves then we won't hold a grudge...

Collective Rebirth

What is the portal of 12th of December,
A day where many will remember...
Why they came here at this time,
The time is perfect and so divine...
Densities clearing from the Earth,
Assisting with a collective rebirth...
Birthing into what, you may ask,
Surrendering to the process is your task...
This time will be a portal to a new way to be,
Where there is plenty of magic to see...
Experiencing life through a new lens,
You will also connect with new friends...
Those that are of the same soul origin,
So your collective mission can begin...
There is no fault in anything you do,
As long as you always stay true to you...
Listen to your own divine guidance,
To activate a full remembrance...

The Irony

How funny is the irony of it all,
The men who judged and made the call...
Saying everyone was out of integrity except themselves,
But they didn't show up, like everyone else...
To me, those who showed up, can be trusted in their word,
It's through their actions, their integrity is heard...
We all made a commitment to dive to the depths,
But their commitment, was not kept....
That to me, shows whose integrity is lacking,
Yet they were the ones, that were attacking...
There was a beautiful opportunity for these men,
To receive the love & support we were all offering...
Yet they let their ego get in the way,
Leaving them out of integrity at the end of the day...
A beautiful lesson, I hope they can see,
Showing them, their lack of integrity...

Gateway Of Grief

That heart wrenching feeling of a loved one passing,
Any past emotions this is definitely surpassing...
You question why is this all happening now,
It just has to be a bad dream somehow...
But it isn't & you realise you're awake,
These waves of grief you cannot shake...
And that is OK to let the tears fall,
It's OK to fall to the floor and simply ball...
Allowing the process & every single feeling,
Is the gateway to your deepest healing...
Honouring the love that you felt for this soul,
Allowing all the memories to take their toll...
Knowing that the love that you felt,
Is the love that will always be dealt...
Even though you can't see their face,
Close your eyes, you may feel them in the space...

A Time Of Giving Presence

It's Christmas Eve, at my family home,
And I want less time, on my phone...
More time being present with what needs to be done,
When I'm being present, any task becomes fun...
Just doing one thing at a time,
I feel the energy of the divine...
There are more than enough hours in the day,
So make sure you include laughter & play...
Because if you spend too much time, always doing,
The magic of life, you will start losing...
So take some time out, and you will see,
You are a gift, & you resting, also serves humanity...
Because everything is energy & it ripples out,
Your business is felt, there is no doubt...
So do yourself a favour, & take time to rest,
Because like you, others want you at your best...
Allow your body to recharge & renew,
And you'll gain extra energy out of the blue...

Christmas Day

It's our Christmas Day in twenty, twenty-two,
And I wonder if Santa was good to you...
Did he treat you well this year,
Did he bring lots of Christmas cheer...
Or were you naughty instead of nice,
If so, next year you better think twice...
Because when we are nice to ourselves,
It ripples out to everyone else...
So what we give is what we get,
Don't do things you will regret...
Treat yourself how you wish to be treated...
Or the same lessons will be repeated...
How can you love yourself even more today,
And not be affected by certain dynamics at play...
Because today we have a choice how we react,
Be aware because it sets the tone for what you will attract...
Set your intentions for what you desire,
Through your actions you will inspire...
Sending love & joy from me to you,
May blessings come to you out of the blue...

Christmas Spirit

You're never too old,
If it's Christmas Spirit you hold...
I'm not sure what others may say,
But joy is yours every single day...
It's not just one day of the year it may appear,
Because Christmas Spirit is love & is always near...
Maybe it comes in the form of a hug,
Maybe it's eggnog in a new mug...
Maybe it's a new toy under the tree,
Maybe it's the joy in others that you see...
I hope you know this spirit is always around,
It's yours to keep once it's been found...
So store the beautiful moments in your heart,
Maybe the moments will inspire some art...
For me, the house is filled with cheer,
Because I have all my family near...

Seeds Of Attachment

What type of attachment style are you,
Does anxiety hit you out of the blue...
If your partner goes away,
Do you create stories regardless of what they say...
Your greatest fear being that they will leave,
You panic and you may struggle to breathe...
Only pushing them away even more,
You end up feeling alone & raw...
In those moments you must allow yourself to feel,
Because the underlying story will reveal...
Where did the story first get created,
Can you see how it plays out with everyone you've dated...
Your inner child didn't get what it needed,
So the unworthiness belief was seeded...
You've spent your life watering that seed,
But what needs to happen for it to be freed...
You need to give that love back to yourself,
Or you'll attract the same pattern in everyone else...
If you want a beautiful flower to grow,
There are new seeds you will need to sow...
It may take time for the seed to sprout,
But maybe that is what life is about...

RACHEL HEANEY

Creating a garden of flowers that like to grow,
Because the flowers show us what we need to know...
Maybe the petals may fall to the floor,
But the plant is still left standing tall...
It may sway a little in the rougher weather,
But with solid foundations it can last forever...
If you water it with love every single day,
It will keep shining even when the sky is grey...

{ 32 }

Creating A Dream

Waking up surrounded by nature & space,
Grateful I trusted my intuition in finding this place...
The sound of birds chirping in the trees,
And the sunshine mixed with fresh air breeze...
Starting my day with meditation & gratitude,
Sets me up with a high vibrational attitude...
Allowing me to focus on the good in everything,
And the beauty every item or thing may bring...
Like this table I am using to write in my book,
I see the finer details as I have a look...
Carvings made saying 'dream' are in the table,
A perfect reminder telling me 'I am able'...
I am able to day dream my reality into existence,
Calling it into the now, not keeping it at a distance...
So I'm dreaming of freedom in all forms,
Because within that dream new realities are born...
And I create my reality each & every day,
So I'm dreaming up more flow & play...
Flow in all forms is alignment for me,
And through that, abundance comes effortlessly...

What Would Love Do

What would love do,
When rejection hits you out of the blue...
It would wrap you up in a comforting hug,
And remind you that you needed to unplug...
That part within that still craves your love,
You connect to it, within and above...
You easily may lose yourself in another,
But I'm reminding you that you are your own lover...
Any rejection is actually an act of kindness,
Showing where you need more mindfulness...
If someone rejects you,
Where do you do it too...
Are you rejecting the things you desire,
So you can flame someone else's fire...
If so, life will throw you off track,
And you don't have time or energy for that...
So don't abandon any part of yourself,
Don't get lost pleasing someone else...
Come back to the union within,
And be open for the magic it will bring...

Self-Motivation

Motivation is my own creation,
Not a specific destination...
Not striving for a place to arrive,
Because I'm here to flow, not barely survive...
Motivation is what lights you up,
What are the things that fill your cup...
That is what you are here to do,
Nothing else will feel more true...
I'm motivated to live in full flow,
Always being guided where to go...
Not getting lost in the doing,
What would that be proving...
I'm motivated to heal my ancestral line,
It happens through me, so the healing is mine...
Allowing everything to be felt through me,
Uncovering more for me to see...
I'm motivated to clear past life karma,
In this life it is my dharma...
So if I don't look motivated to you,
This is clearly the work you're not being called to do...

Energy Speaks

The energy speaks louder to me,
Than any actions will have me see...
Energy is a language I know and speak,
It allows me to find the answers I seek...
If someone's energy is not clear,
The message in the energy will appear...
It's truly a gift to be able to feel so much,
I feel the energy before there is touch...
So if the intention doesn't feel good energetically,
I'll say no & step away effortlessly...
Because I can feel energy from a distance,
I feel when there is any sort of resistance...
I also feel when people are in their heart,
Remember that love is a form of art...

Deeper Trust

How much deeper can I surrender and trust,
The pain of holding on was getting too much...
I kept hearing the words 'everything needs to go',
And I'm reminded to trust and drop into full flow,
Because the energy will never lie,
So trust all to which you align...
I've been initiated into a deeper level of what I'm here to teach,
For me, it comes in the surrender, and not what people preach...
As I watched, and let go of every piece,
I knew I'd soon feel that sense of relief...
Letting go creates the space,
There may be fears you need to face...
But the thing I've been shown over and over again,
Life rewards me, when I trust & follow the guidance of when...
This is always beyond what makes logical sense,
There may be moments in the void of suspense...
But life has a plan you can't yet see,
And surrendering and trusting may be the key...

Rewards Of Letting Go

You're always rewarded for letting go,
Not being scared of what you don't know...
Because if something doesn't feel right,
You no longer need to hold on tight...
Because it's exhausting to keep that grip,
And parts of you, will start to rip...
Surrender, as you'll be caught in the fall,
But letting go, is always your call...
Your dreams may hold the clues, to all you desire,
So trust, and then, you will truly inspire...
People will feel that courage from you,
And it will draw them in too...
You'll become magnetic & you will see,
That you create your own reality...
So is it one that sets your soul on fire,
Where you are attracting all you desire...

{ 38 }

Intuition Makes No Sense

Intuition makes no sense to the logical mind,
So it's there the answers cannot be found...
When you're guided to go a certain way,
You must trust what the whispers say...
When you think you can't trust any more,
Remember, relying on your ego is a chore...
Can you drop back into the feeling,
Maybe there is land that needs healing...
So follow the path and where it leads,
Maybe down the creek & through the reeds...

Lured In

Be aware of the businesses that lure you in,
A massive commitment of debt will begin...
They may want you signed up for a full year,
And your bank balance will totally clear...
I've fallen for this many times,
And now I'll see what comes in these rhymes...
It was a pattern I thought another could help me clear,
But they just want the money, not to help with your fear...
I'm here to help people to trust,
Being discerning is a must...
Never will I force people to buy from me,
And I also won't sell my soul for free...

Ultimate Duality

Dancing in and out of each polarity,
It's the ultimate form of duality...
Moments of action to get things done,
Then surrendering to have some fun...
Balancing my feminine flowing,
With my masculine knowing...
Guiding me through the day,
In the most balanced way...
When I listen to the subtle feeling within me,
I'm guided so effortlessly...
And when I follow each sign,
I'm constantly aligned with the divine...
And that is what I'm here to do,
To live a life of balanced flow, it's true...

Not Open To Receive

As the full moon sets in the sky,
You may ask yourself questions of why...
Why could someone not receive your love,
It was the greatest gift from above...
But not everyone knows how to receive,
Or maybe they were taught not to believe...
It's too good to be true they may say,
So they push it away the very next day...
They may be numb to all they're feeling,
And may want to run from what starts revealing...
Maybe they need time & space all alone,
Through their minds they like to roam...
Keeping busy so they don't feel too much,
But what they really want is your loving touch...
However, they've never got what they desired,
It was just a thought that they admired...
But living in the head isn't for you,
You know you deserve a love so true...
So entertaining a connection like this,
Is not going to have you in a state of bliss...

What Is Real

What is this life, is it even real,
It's all an illusion I'm starting to feel...
But am I asleep or awake,
What is real and what is fake...
If I create my reality each day,
I need to be careful what I say...
I only focus on what I desire,
And through the energy I inspire...
Being free to flow where I'm guided to go,
Following my full body yes and also the no...
It really is as simple as that,
I don't ever need to come from lack...

# Energy Of The Tree

Guided down the creek I kept walking,
Hearing the energy of the tree calling...
It was calling to me,
I couldn't yet see...
But when I turned the corner, it was in my vision,
And there was no having to make a decision...
Because I knew I was right where I was meant to be,
This tree had wisdom & energy to share with me...
The energy came through so strong,
I knew I was right where I belong...

That Off Feeling

Something doesn't quite feel right,
I woke suddenly in the night...
The energy felt like something was wrong,
And out of nowhere, the rain came along...
Pouring down so strong, straight away,
Something felt off, with what's at play...
Are more floods predicted, for this time,
Or are they man made, as such a crime...
Putting people's lives at risk, to gain control,
They don't even care about the death toll...
Earthquakes & floods like never before,
The rain keeps coming, more and more...
Be prepared, as much as you can,
Your own sovereignty, you must be a fan...
Know that everything will be OK,
Just stay true to you, every single day...

In The Silence

She hears the whispers of the Earth,
Letting her know, what wants to birth...
The land holding her as she walks the way,
Guided so effortlessly, every single day...
Her bare feet kissing the ground below,
With every step, the whispers grow...
"This way", she hears, calling from the trees,
Even more beauty, which brings her to her knees...
She bows in reverence of the beauty all around,
And feels the message in every single sound...
Sometimes it's in the silence, that we hear,
And we know, there is nothing to fear...
An invitation to tune into the subtle call,
And allow nature to hold you, as you fall...
"Fall from where", you may ask,
Surrender and trust, is your task...
Then the next step will be shown,
Knowing you're always guided, and not alone...

In Full Flow Effect

A massive cycle is coming to an end,
A deep dive within, so my heart would mend...
What a journey it has been,
So many gifts, I am now seeing...
Heart being cracked open, to more light,
I just had to surrender, and also write...
Because, hidden between the words, on these pages,
Was guidance, to help me through all the stages...
I wonder what book I will release next,
Will it be spoken word, or will it be text...
Will people feel the wisdom, within the lines,
Maybe they will read it, multiple times...
Or will they learn to trust themselves more,
Will they live in flow, rather than, life as a chore...

{ 47 }

Heart Expansion

It was the two-year celebration for C2BC,
And they did a beautiful honoring of me...
The journey that was guided by our higher selves,
So we could birth a movement, to support everyone else...
To see over a thousand, turn up in the space,
Bought gratitude, as tears rolled down my face...

Honour Self

Can you honour & respect yourself, over all others,
This includes your family, friends, and your lovers...
Sometimes it's hard to say "no" to another,
What if you hurt your sister or brother...
But if you keep giving, to everyone else,
You'll have no energy, left for yourself...
Your life force will be lacking,
And things will start cracking...
I am always tested, with not abandoning me,
Because, for so long, this lesson, I couldn't see...
I thought, if everyone was happy, so was I,
So above all else, that was my why...
But when I saw that wasn't, authentically me,
I had to set, that people pleaser, free...
Because, if it's not a full yes, it is a no,
So I trust the guidance, if I'm to go...
Because, when I give myself, what I need,
Any past patterns, can be freed...
Allowing me to be, in alignment each day,
With what my intuition, has to say...

Authentic Leadership

I'm being called, to lead the way,
Not by copying what others do, and say...
But, by walking a path, others can't see,
Where I'm in flow, and feeling so free...
Calling in those, who aren't motivated by money,
Some people out there, may think, that's kind of funny...
But I am not coming, from a place of lack,
Because I don't hustle, it doesn't mean I'm slack...
I work on doing, what I love,
Always listening to guidance, from above...
As when I trust the whispers, that come in,
Is when true freedom, starts to begin...
Then my vibration is higher & I easily attract what I desire,
And my mission is to lead, and to also inspire...
I've been doing this for over ten years now,
And I've journeyed all the others, somehow...
But I've realised, that it is my mission,
To teach others, to listen to their intuition...
So they can flow through life, with ease & grace,
And have a solid foundation of trust, as their base...

Magic Moments

Do you notice, that when you align,
You'll be sent a message, from the divine...
A sprinkle of magic, to cheer you on,
Letting you know, you're where you belong...
When you notice these moments of love,
More will be sent, from above...
Confirmation, you're on the right track,
Life letting you know; it's got your back...
Because you're listening, and trusting,
There is nothing, that needs adjusting...
Take note of these little things,
And the joy & heart expansion, it brings...
As your soul lights up, like this,
You'll be open, to share more bliss...
And you'll activate others, to feel it too,
Staying in flow, is all, you have to do...

{ 51 }

Highest Good Of All

What is for the highest good of all,
It's to allow any control to fall...
In the stillness the answers are found,
And through alignment, they will ground...
The feeling in the body is the cue,
For all your dreams, to come true...
Trust all that is being asked of you,
And don't let fear stop what is true...
It may not make sense to the mind,
But so much more magic you will find...
Stress doesn't need to be in yourself,
And you'll then inspire everyone else...
So may you have the courage to live in flow,
Always guided where to go...
Magic in every moment is available to you,
Give yourself permission to be open to it too...

Letting Go Of The Grip

Is there something you are holding on to,
If there is, I'll tell you what you have to do...
Let go and trust what's meant for you, will find you,
It's the hardest, yet simplest thing to do...
Surrender it all to the divine,
And what's for you will align...
Because holding on takes energy,
And creates a needy density...
One that is coming from lack,
So lack is what you'll then attract...
And to attract all that you desire,
There are past stories to rewire...
You are safe, you are loved & you are enough,
I know letting go of the grip can be tough...
But you will be rewarded along the way,
When you listen to what this poem has to say...
Call all your energy back to yourself,
You don't need to seek anything from anyone else...
You are love in its purest form,
So let self-love become your norm...

Divine Plan

Life has a plan you may not be able to see,
And there are things that need to be set free...
So what is it that you're scared to let go,
Know, that is what is keeping you out of flow...
Because it illuminates a distrust within yourself,
And that will ripple out to everyone else...
Deep down you know what you need to do,
It's the key to build that trust back within you...
You didn't come here to play safe & keep small,
You came to follow your truth and the call...
The call comes from a place within,
And ignoring it, is the sin...
So find some space alone to tune in,
And listen to the guidance on where to begin...

This Moment

All we ever have is this moment now,
Everything else fades away somehow...
So how present can you be,
Allowing the energy to flow free...
Because if you are not in your mind,
It's the magic of this moment, you will find...
So may you attract others to this place,
Where it's just pure presence, that you face...
The mind not robbing this moment in time,
Where to magic moments, you do align...
You decide to live, one moment at a time,
Because that's when you feel the divine...
And you come to be a channel for that too,
So you are able to feel what is true...
You decide to let fear melt away,
You decide to let in magic every day...
You allow love to flow through your being,
Knowing you're loved, and safe to be seen...

Inner Union

You recognize your inner masculine,
Now seeing your inner feminine...
It is the reunion you've been waiting for,
You couldn't have wished for anything more...
You needed this space to be on your own,
Your inner temple you needed to roam...
To face all the parts you'd been rejecting,
And forgive the parts that you were projecting...
You now love and accept all parts of you,
Even the parts you never thought you'd be able to...
You're now a stable base for yourself,
And can also be that for everyone else...
Leading the way for others to breakthrough,
Finding love within yourself, was what you had to do...
Creating a safe space of healing for another,
And also attracting in your own divine lover...
Because they have met themselves in the depths too,
So you both met each other in a love so true...

Void Of Change

Do you know what comes with change,
It's the void feeling before things rearrange...
Where you don't know where you're to be,
And the vision is now not clear to see...
It's in these moments your trust is needed,
Your dreams have already been seeded...
This is a very familiar place for me,
One that I can now sit in comfortably...
Life has a plan greater than you may know,
So just breathe, relax and let life flow...
Things are unfolding in divine time,
Rearranging so things will align...
To put you on your highest path,
Trusting in the magic is your task...

Worthy Of Love

Watching the waves rolling in,
As the waters start stirring within...
The waters were inviting your tears,
Surrendering any of those fears...
But what was the fear even about, you ask,
Just surrendering & allowing, was your task...
Not trying to understand with your mind,
Because the answer you would never find...
Maybe it felt like a sadness for your heart,
And the journey it's had, from the start...
Wondering what it would feel like, to let love in,
But you have a block, so it isn't able to begin...
Blocking the thing you crave at your core,
Are you too needy to want someone to adore...
Why must you have an object of your affection,
Does it keep you heading in the right direction...
Or does it make you feel not enough,
And like you're not worthy of love...

Redirection

A lot can change in the blink of an eye,
A redirection to what you align...
So be brave and trust this day,
And all the magic coming your way...
You've outgrown old versions of yourself,
And you've gained an abundance of wealth...
It's now time to open your heart and receive,
It will be better than you can ever believe...
You were brave and shared what was true,
And it's also perfect if they couldn't meet you...
Because you're not on the same vibration anymore,
Even if in your heart, its them you'll always adore...
The rejection doesn't affect you anymore,
Your heart keeps opening more and more...
It's up to you if you are ready to open to love,
You can choose that timeline, is what I hear from above...
Can you release control and surrender to the flow,
Of the love that will heal you more than you know...

Speak Your Truth

The thing you least want to speak, is the thing that'll set you free,
Ask yourself why would I want to keep those words caged in me...
What is the fear that is holding you back,
That exact fear is what is keeping you off track...
Let this be a reminder that you have a choice,
You do have the courage to use your voice...

# Purpose

Our purpose and mission are why we are here,
There is first the conditioning that needs to clear...
To open to what we are here to share,
It's our mission and should be held with care...
One step with what action is needed,
The plan has already been seeded...

Don't Ignore The Call

She felt the call the venture out to the poetry night,
She was there to listen to another, not be in full sight...
Because she hadn't yet done a live reading from her book,
She is still feeling the vulnerability, having a book took...
Speaking her poetry in a room full of strangers,
Had her ego mind creating all sorts of dangers...
What if the words won't speak,
What if people think her poetry is weak...
What if her voice shakes & tears fall,
And into a dark hole she wants to crawl...
It's safer to just stay nestled into the couch in the corner,
As she's not an amazing poetry performer...
So she didn't put her name down on the list,
The opportunity to face her fear, she had just missed...
In a way this felt ultra-safe,
But it's the fear she's being guided to face...
Near the end of the night, they had room for one more,
Her heart was racing, and she was hearing the call...
She put her hand up, despite the fear,
She was ready for it, to disappear...
But they chose another instead of she,
As she sunk back into the couch's safety...

Divinely Aligned

Not been chosen was her familiar place,
But she was done and over that space...
She was then annoyed she didn't put her name down on the list,
This initiation, she had reluctantly just missed...
She realised that maybe there were messages in her words that people needed to hear,
So when the next poetry night presents, she will be clear...
She'll share the words that want to be spoken,
And remind herself, she is not broken...

Let Love In

Can you choose to let love in,
Where do you even begin...
It comes down to you not feeling worthy of love,
Even though it was why you were sent from above...
It's safer for you to go for the partners that aren't open,
They run from any words of love that are spoken...
And they are a reflection of you,
You now may see, you do that too...
Your heart will open and pour out so much love,
'Drip feed it, not fire hose it' you now hear from above...
Because as you now see, when it's not familiar in our body,
Or where we weren't shown how to embody...
It can feel like danger to open and trust,
So the ego says, 'running is a must'...
And running will ultimately keep us safe,
From the vulnerability we would have to face...
So maybe you were unconsciously fire hosing them,
So they would run, and you'd be safe again...
This may be a lot, to have truly land,
Once you see the pattern, you'll fully understand...

Glimpse In Their Eyes

Connections beyond the mind,
Where the answers you will find...
You'll feel a spark from when you meet,
And maybe you'll want to bow at their feet...
But life has a plan that you'll eventually see,
If you trust & follow the guidance so clearly...
Soul contracts for meeting each other,
Again, they don't have to be a lover...
Just a glimpse in their eyes,
It's a recognition with no disguise...
The mystery is what role they will play,
When you listen to the words that they say...
Synchronicities will guide the way,
Always trusting the energy at play...

Abundance Is Energy

When I left school, I couldn't wait to earn money,
I look back now and think, that's kind of funny...
I was always striving for more,
To live a life that I adore...
But life back then was keeping busy, to numb my pain,
Escaping with partying, so the pain wouldn't remain...
Of course, it would still be hidden within me,
But I kept so busy, as a way to feel free...
What a journey life has taken me on,
To uncover truths, and my own soul song...
I woke again with this dream & vision I always see,
Where abundance is energy & we all feel so free...
Not seeking the next way to make a sale,
Because that model, will eventually fail...
If your worth is based on how much money you make,
I invite you to give, instead of just take...
I've been observing this pattern online,
Where people promote money as a way to shine...
I know we do need money in this day & age,
But be careful it doesn't keep you in a cage...
Trapped in a system, full of greed,
Maybe these words will plant a seed...

Divinely Aligned

Your energy is your greatest gift,
That is what can help the consciousness shift...
Last year I fell into investing the greatest fee,
And wow, was it the greatest lesson for me...
I signed up as I wanted to share more of my gifts,
To support people going through energy shifts...
I soon saw the manipulation that was at play,
My body said 'no', to following their guidance every day...
Even though I'd invested so much,
I fell out of alignment & was falling out of touch...
Everything they were teaching, made me feel ill,
I chose to exit out, in my own free will...
I still had to pay, but honoured myself,
Because that is what I'm here to teach everyone else...
I see this vision, of how life could be,
When we use our gifts, to exchange freely...
Abundance of energy, in all forms,
Community coming together, through the storms...
Maybe there is someone who likes to cook,
And would love a massage, for the energy it took...
Maybe there are people out there who truly care,
I wonder what they are here to share...
Without always striving to make a higher wage,
If we came together, we'd support each other, through every stage...
So I wonder who sees this vision too,
Where we live, and act from what feels true...

{ 65 }

Give & Receive In Full Flow

I keep waking in the night with the same message coming through,
I'm being shown the steps, of what I have to do...
I first got this message, many years ago,
But the time is now, they want us to know...
Things are changing before our eyes,
The way we've been controlled, no longer in disguise...
Many that I know, have seen this for a while,
And could see it all, coming from a mile...
We need to take back our power as a community,
And build new way, with the power of unity...
Many are dreaming of a time, living off the land,
The importance of this, people are starting to understand...
Where money isn't something that keeps us stuck,
Feeling we are constantly hit, with another mac truck...
I've been here in the past, allowing bills & rates to get in the way,
Of what my intuition, was guiding me to do each day...
That is just being a slave, to the power at be,
But true freedom comes, when we choose sovereignty...
There are many who know, they are here to support this change,
To help lead the way, as things rearrange...
We know it is part of our mission, and why we came,
So we can support the people, so suffering won't remain...

Divinely Aligned

I want to make sure people can get, the support they need,
And are not always faced with obstacles, of money & greed...
Let's start to support each other, without the need for money,
In this day and age, you might think that sounds kind of funny...
And yes, there are things we still need to pay for,
But what if we could also live a life, we truly adore...
8 years ago, when I got into massage and healing,
I'll tell you the thing, that seemed most appealing...
It was being able to do energy exchanges, without having to pay,
We just get to do what we love, every single day...
Not only giving, but receiving too,
Self-care doesn't have to be, a rarity for you...
We all have our own unique gifts to share,
And when given, we can also receive self-care...
I know many of us give, and struggle to receive,
And I know you might find it, hard to believe...
But when you receive, you also give,
And that can be, the most nourishing way to live...
Maybe you haven't treated yourself, in too long,
You've let lack of money, make it feel wrong...
What if you could be part of community, that are open for energy exchanges,
To support your fellow community, through any of life's stages...
Maybe you wish for someone, with a certain skill,
But you wonder, how you'd even pay the bill...
Maybe you hold a gift, that person may need,
When energy exchanged, the bills & debt can be freed...
Think of all the things you pay money for,
And how an energy exchange will help you live a life you adore...
If you are feeling the call to start exchanging like this,
Reach out to your community, so you can live in bliss...
It's important we are supported, during these times,
Feeling nurtured & nourished, as your community aligns...

Blooming Of The Rose

Like a flower, before it's in full bloom,
There might be darkness, like no full moon...
Where you can't see the light, in the depths,
But deep down you know that the tears that you wept...
Are the nourishment, to water the seed that you are,
At times it may seem never ending, and so far...
But trust me, I know, it's part of how we grow,
There will be times, where you have nowhere to go...
Make peace with being in this place,
Enjoy the solitude, of your own sacred space...
Nestled into the womb, of Mother Earth,
You're going through your own divine rebirth...
You can't rush the blooming of the Rose,
But your surrendering helps, as it grows...
So find that light within,
And trust the process to begin...
Soon the light will guide you to open,
Be mindful of all the words, that are spoken...

Conscious Awareness

Have you ever felt triggered and let down,
Where there is part of you that wanted to leave town...
Maybe someone in your life wasn't true to their word,
So you were left feeling very unseen, and unheard...
You could feel their untruth when it was spoken,
Your inner lie detector had been awoken...
And in that moment instead of calling them out,
You abandoned self, to give them the benefit of the doubt...
What a beautiful lesson of trusting yourself,
When you feel the untruth spoken by someone else...
You want people's truth and nothing less,
Without it, your friendship is meaningless...
But with conscious awareness & open hearts,
You'll both be able to own both your parts...
And come back to the love that you are,
Not allowing past stories to take you far...

{ 68 }

Rainbow Bridge

There is a rainbow bridge from heaven to Earth,
It will help you in this time of rebirth...
Remembering you are an activator of the bridge,
And it can also be amplified by the didge...
Allowing a tunnel of light to show the way,
And give clear guidance every single day...
The rainbow bridge is also the kundalini rising,
They may have seemed different but now no disguising...
The base of the spine being the same as Earth,
And the crown being the portal of rebirth...
The chakras as the stairs of the rainbow,
Holding the keys to everything you'll ever know...
Each colour holding lessons & initiations,
Guiding you through every creation...
Allowing the path to be clear,
As you let go of any fear...
Your base finding its own stability,
Your sacral activating your creativity...
Your solar igniting the power within,
Your heart allowing a new level of love to begin...
Your throat speaking words of wisdom,
Your third eye expanding your vision...

Divinely Aligned

Your crown connecting you to the divine,
Once all activated, you divinely align...
This journey can seem like a rough ride,
It's to your inner compass you must abide...
Allowing it to guide the way,
By listening to your soul whispers each day...

{ 69 }

Physical Upgrade

Our bodies are going through a physical upgrade,
From above, the plan has already been made...
It's about surrendering & allowing the purge to take place,
There will be people we won't be able to face...
New doors will open out of the blue,
When you're in alignment, with you...
Your mind may have created a plan,
And your soul may not be a fan...
But maybe it is the other way around...
There's a soul plan, but the ego doesn't want it found...

{ 70 }

Wishes

May your wishes come true,
May blessings come out of the blue...
What if today you honoured yourself,
Looking after you, instead of everyone else...
Would you feel the massive shift,
And know, you're helping the consciousness uplift...
Or would you push on, and feel broken,
Because you ignored the inner guidance, that was spoken...
How can you nourish 'you' every day,
By listening to what your soul whispers say...

Soul Journey

Following the whispers, following the call,
Allowing what doesn't serve you, to fall...
Creating the space for what you're calling in,
And all the magical blessings it will bring...
The ways you've leapt into the unknown,
And all that you've been shown...
The hurts, the pains, all played their part,
And they all helped in cracking open your heart...
Cracking it open to let the light and love in,
So your greatest soul mission, could begin...
As you're here to illuminate the way,
By listening to what the soul whispers say...
Guided by, and in service to the divine,
What is for you, you will align...

Beyond The Body

When they say, "time is an illusion", what do they mean,
It means, all versions of you, also exist in the unseen...
Not in the past, or another lifetime,
But right now, is where you align...
Multi-dimensional, yet all happening now,
It's hard for our human mind to understand somehow...
But when you realise you are nothing, and everything,
You will feel the freedom, that it can bring...
Moment to moment, we create our reality,
And experience this planet of polarity...
You can journey through all parts of yourself,
And even feel connection with everyone else...
Because we are all part of this cosmic thread,
Remembering our divinity that was embed...
Embers sparking the remembrance of this,
The breath is a gateway you don't want to miss...
Something we do every day without a thought,
But when done consciously, there is wisdom, you'll be taught...
Every day, awakening more at your core,
You'll realise beyond this physical body, there is so much more...

You Hold The Key

How much do you ignore the little things,
The subtleties and the message it brings...
It might just seem like no big deal,
But eventually the pain it will reveal...
So what truth needs to be spoken,
What part of you has been awoken...
The energy doesn't lie so pay attention,
As you walk your path of ascension...
There will be people & things that will try hold you back,
But you can decide if you're still coming from lack...
Know your worth & honour what feels good to you,
Then you'll live a life that feels so true...
Don't get lost seeking outside of yourself,
Because you already hold the greatest wealth...
It's you, it always has been, you hold the key,
The key to unlock, and set yourself free...

{ 74 }

Journey Of Self-Acceptance

You've felt so much joy being in your human suit,
For so long you wanted a new body to recruit...
But you've learnt to accept, and love yourself,
And with that, you feel love for everyone else...
Life feels and looks more delicious than ever before,
And when you look at you, you truly adore...
All that you've moved through in your years,
All the pain and all the tears...
You were paving a path of healing,
Each step finally revealing...

{ 75 }

Love As My Guide

Today I celebrate my Mum & Dad,
And the 50 years of marriage they've now had...
Life bought them together at a young age,
And together they grew through every stage...
I'm sure there were challenges they faced along the way,
But they chose to love, every single day...
I'm getting teary as I write this now,
Wondering how I got so lucky somehow...
I'm grateful they didn't stop at two,
They saved the best for last, it's true...
Three daughters & four granddaughters too,
For us all, there is nothing they wouldn't do...
Their love is felt far and wide,
They show me what it's like with love by your side...
For those that know them, know they have hearts of gold,
And when around them, fun is always ready to unfold...
There is always laughter to be had,
When in the company of my Mum & Dad...
It's so beautiful to be a part of this life they created,
They were just 15 & 17 when they first dated...
They inspire me to choose love, every day,
Despite what fear may have to say...

Divinely Aligned

They volunteer their time to Sailability,
Helping people to sail who have a disability...
They help them to spend time at sea,
Being surrounded by water, where they feel so free...
They give so much of their love that's overflowing,
Which has others lift up and always glowing...
I have so much love & admiration for my Mum & Dad,
For having them as my parents, I am so glad...

{ 76 }

Mind Battle

The mind is a fascinating thing,
With all the stories it can create within...
But who created them really,
It was us, which is so silly...
When we realise every story, we've ever created,
Has attracted the match, for those we've dated...
So if you created the story of unworthiness,
Then you can also clear that craziness...
You can create a new story, as simple as that,
What your mind thinks, you then attract...

Desire To Be Met

We've been taught relationships are easy,
But going to the depths isn't aways breezy...
You get that some don't want to be fully met,
Because they've never experienced it yet...
They don't know the expansion that takes place,
When the inner demons they are brave to face...
And sometimes you can only do so much by yourself,
Before your evolution requires a mirror from someone else...
You don't want to settle for anything less than being seen,
Being seen and held in all your being...
The parts of you that may seem scary to share,
Because you have to make sure the other really does care...
If there isn't a stable foundation as the base,
You won't feel fully safe with them in the space...
And this will give them a choice,
To run away, or use their voice...
To communicate what they are feeling,
And what the mirror is revealing...
If they can meet you in this place,
Then a devotional reflection they will face...
As you will devote to them if they can truly meet you,
Be brave as their heart opens, is what they'll have to do...

So Simple

It's really simple and sometimes you may forget,
Enjoy now, instead of what you don't have yet...
Life knows exactly what you're calling in,
When in alignment, the universe will bring...
All your hearts yearnings, and desires,
Because your frequency is what inspires...
Life is creating from the energy you bring,
So you must stay positive from within...
You know all of this,
But sometimes you miss...
You miss the simplicity of this existence,
Which is then what created all the resistance...

{ 79 }

It's Already Yours

Everything you desire is already within you,
Others just show up so you can clearly see...
That they reflect where you may come from lack,
So you can get back on the right track...
Easily flowing when you are devoted to yourself,
Not trying to seek love from anyone else...
Because hoping for another is saying you're not enough,
This realization is one that can be tough...
Showing us that any seeking for something outside,
Is never going to be, trust me, I've tried...
Become magnetic by being true to you,
By only accepting what feels true...
Knowing that all you desire is already yours,
It's a universal law, and it always keeps scores...
Magic exists in every single moment,
You'll miss it if you are not present...
So come back to this moment now,
Where all your desires exist somehow...

Effortless Flow

Every moment we have a choice,
We are creating with our mind and voice...
So if there is something that doesn't feel right,
Trust the feeling, the current, you don't have to fight...
Because to flow through your day,
Is your choice, when you choose which way...
Do you go upstream, always feeling depleted,
Or do you surrender to the flow you've been greeted...
Do whatever lights you up,
That is what will fill your cup...
It's the true power of being in flow,
Where your vibration takes you, where you're to go...
Your desires effortlessly flow to you,
When you live a life so true...
Focus on what feels good within,
And allow the momentum to begin...
Flowing you in the right direction,
Now you've done a course correction...

Existence

What is the point of it all,
From where did we fall...
Were we sent to figure it out,
Is that what this experience is about...
Maybe it's just to love what is now,
Is that the whole point somehow...
What if nature showed us who we are,
Reminded us we never have to go far...
To feel the peace within,
Is an easy place to begin...
Just accept that all is perfect,
Some thoughts we may need to eject...
We never have to do a certain thing,
Allow the peace that thought can bring...
Find the satisfaction to have fun,
You don't have to get anything done...
What if you can enjoy yourself every day,
It would be the greatest game you could play...
And you came here to play and create,
Then you'll align to your greatest fate...

{ 82 }

Life Responds To Vibration

Life responds to your vibration,
It's the foundation of your creation...
So are you creating a stable base,
By creating from aligned space...
Everything mirrors back what you've called in,
So checking in on how you feel, is how you begin...
Your inner being is your pilot through day-to-day life,
Looking after your inner being, will keep you out of strife...
So what is important to you,
Is it to live a life that feels true...
We are constantly creating our reality,
Through our inner and outer duality...
What makes you feel lit up,
That is what will fill your cup...
It's just you, that matters now,
Focus good on you and life will reward you somehow...
Your inner being is your life force,
So you want to keep it on course...
Do and focus on what you love,
That is the message from above...

{ 83 }

Be Happy

Just be happy, and life will reflect it back,
When you're happy, you are on the right track...
The universe knows who you are,
And will guide you from afar...
To align you with who you're meant to meet,
Always seeing who you are to greet...
Anything is possible if you trust,
Trusting what lights you up, is a must...
We create everything we desire,
Our passion is our fuel to inspire...

Momentum Of Flow

Have you ever felt the momentum of flow,
Where you're in alignment and you know...
Life feels so magic and satisfying,
As you're noticing all you are aligning...
Joy and bliss emanate your entire being,
And beauty in everything you are seeing...
The logical mind doesn't stand a chance,
Because you're in an energetic trance...
Where life is manifesting your desires,
Your high vibration is what inspires...
Stay in this feeling as long as you can,
And keep coming back to it again & again...
Creating in a space of what you love,
And you'll be rewarded from above...

{ 85 }

Simply Live

Life really can be so simple, it's true,
And there is just one thing, you have to do...
It's doing what lights you up,
Doing the things that fill your cup...
Because when you're topped up, you can overflow,
Allowing the energy to flow, where it's to go...
And in that flowing,
There is a divine knowing...
You've become magnetic in multiple ways,
And you're being rewarded multiple days...
Life gets to be this good,
For so long, many have misunderstood...
And as they start experiencing this,
They realise they can live, in a state of bliss...

{ 86 }

Divinity Of Flow

All you have to do, is to know you're in full flow,
And your inner being will guide you where to go...
Because you've forever been planting seeds along the way,
Trusting that they will be ready, to sprout one day...
You're now reaping the rewards of those seeds planted long ago,
And it's allowing you to now, live in full flow...
Flowers don't grow overnight,
It won't happen in your sight...
So when you continue to live,
More seeds of life you will give...
There comes a certain moment in time,
Where the growth from the seed, you now align...
It's such a journey, and not about the destination,
Just pave your way, with intentional creation...
By intentional, I mean, doing what you love,
That is the guidance from above...

{ 87 }

Your Guide Through Life

You are your own spiritual guide,
It's your own inner compass, you must abide...
Because every time you do follow your inner being,
It's all the signs and synchronicities, you will be seeing...
Showing you, you're back in alignment within,
And this is what makes your soul truly sing...
Connected, tuned in, and turned on,
Is where we all, long to belong...
After years of dancing between the duality,
You've now seen so clearly, you create your reality...
You always have, and you always will,
So all your desires, will easily fulfil...
The universe aligning you with all you desire,
When you follow your bliss, you will inspire...
And abundance will continue to flow,
Because you're always guided where to go...

{ 88 }

Sun Lover

I miss you when you're not around,
You're the greatest lover I've ever found...
From the moment my eyes caught your sight,
You've reminded me to shine so bright...
Sometimes I'll be walking on my own,
And I feel you surprise me, as I moan...
A sigh of relief as your warmth touches my skin,
You make me melt, from deep within...
Wrapped up in your embrace,
Has me move with such grace...
Then all of a sudden, you may disappear,
And then nothing, seems as clear...
Because when you're around, you light the way,
Filling me with gratitude, through the day...
When you're gone, I miss you, but know you'll be back,
Without you, I'm not as stable, on this track...
I know absence makes the heart grow fonder,
And my love for you, grows even stronger...
But I love waking up to you,
It's my favourite thing in the world to do...
Allowing you to shine the light, so I can see,
That you make this Sun Goddess, feel so free...

Momentum Of Flowing

When you feel the momentum, it's time to act,
Because that vibration, is when you'll attract...
All the things you've always wished for,
All the things you didn't know you'd adore...
But the universe has been keeping score,
And always ready to provide you with so much more...
Yet you just weren't dropping into full flow,
So your manifestations had nowhere to go...
But now you understand that feeling,
And what life is effortlessly revealing...
Life is always working in the unseen,
Especially when you are just being...
So make sure you have days with no plan,
And deeply listen to the whispers, if you can...
They will guide you on your way,
Especially when you listen & trust everyday...

{ 90 }

Internal Validation

Are you always seeking guidance or approval from someone else,
If so, you must know, validation can only come from yourself...
So take this as a sign, it's time to look within,
Where did this need for validation begin...
As a kid did you never feel good enough for your Mum or Dad,
Maybe whatever you did, you got in trouble for being bad...
Now you walk through life, not wanting to do anything wrong,
And you're constantly feeling, like you don't belong...
I'm here to remind you to let go of the story playing in your mind,
Be present in this moment and internal validation you will find...

Secret To Life

Giving is receiving when it's in full flow,
Does this make sense or do you want to know...
If you're always in full flow,
You will also be guided where to go...
Maybe there is someone you're guided to,
And they will receive a gift from you...
In this moment you're divinely aligned,
So the gift of giving you will find...
Life is always giving to you as you flow,
You're lit up by life and it will show...
You'll attract all that you desire,
And will also give the gift to inspire...
Life gets to be enjoyed each day,
Your seeds were planted, now it's time to play...
You've created a playground that continues to grow,
The hard work is done, now you truly know...
The secret to life and why you're here,
And it isn't just about your mission or career...
It's about being in vibrational alignment,
To get there you'll need to master discernment...
And also be tapped into your feeling,
And the subtlety that it's revealing...

Attraction Or Distraction

There is always a reason for attraction,
Maybe you're both looking for a distraction...
Instead of loving yourself,
You seek love from someone else...
Maybe you abandon yourself to another,
Because it's self-love you're yet to discover...
And maybe all of a sudden it all makes sense,
And you see the gift of their absence...
Showing you where you're not being true to you,
Now you know what you get to do...
You get to drop back in your own flow,
Where there is nothing you need to know...
You're at your happiest when aligned,
So no longer will you stay blind...
Trust what is a full body yes,
The law of attraction will sort the rest...

{ 93 }

Chi Chats

I caught up with my dear friend today,
There was so much we got to say...
Things we hadn't said before,
Inspiring thoughts came more and more...
We were activating each other for our next steps,
Clearing out any abundance debts...
Because we get to do what we love,
That was always the message from above...
We don't need to do anything other than what lights us up,
Because that will fill up our energy cup...
Then we will be living in the overflow,
And that's when the energy knows where to go...
To align us with our high vibration,
We are gifted with our own creation...
We deep down know all of this,
That we can live in a state of bliss...
Not needing to lean into resistance,
It's our choice what we call into existence...
So if anything was possible, what would we do,
We'd live our life doing what feels true...
Each moment trusting what lights us up,
Not choosing the things when our bodies say 'nup'...

Monkey In Your Mind

Do you allow freedom to the monkey in your mind,
If so, it's likely there will be chaos you will find...
Your thoughts create your reality,
So is it needing more clarity...
Clarity around what is showing up each day,
Are you happy with what your thoughts may say...
Or do you need to set some boundaries,
Or maybe just go 'off with the fairies'...
They make you think that fairies are bad,
But has there ever been a fairy that made you sad...
For me they take me to a peaceful place,
And there is no monkey in that space...
So my thoughts are pure and clear,
And I'm not in a state of fear...
So if you can get into a daydream,
You'll start to feel so serene...
How do you do it you ask,
Just be present is your only task...
Look around at what you can see,
Observe an object as you just be...
I love to do this with a flower or tree,
It's the gateway to set the monkey mind free...

{ 95 }

Freedom For The Brave

When the whispers come, I know I must trust,
Trust in the guidance and have courage is a must...
This life of freedom is for the brave,
You'll be rewarded with all you crave...
Not crave in the lack mentality,
Because your vibration is what creates your reality...
Some may not want to own what they attracted,
And the thought is one they have rejected...
But it's true what the wise ones say,
Our vibe attracts our tribe, every day...
So if you don't like what you're seeing,
Changing your vibration will be so freeing...
How do you do that, you may ask,
Improving your thoughts, is your task...
Practice until it's easy to do,
You'll then feel as life rewards you...

Packing Up

The cleanup of my home space,
This has been a magical place...
Allowing me to birth so much,
And share my gifts through touch...
But life was guiding me to let go,
And I must trust, to live in flow...
Every little whisper is guiding me,
All the magic I continue to see...
The synchronicities let me know I'm on track,
I become magnetic, and easily attract...
This is a secret that not many know,
If only they'd trust where they're guided to go...
I've spent ten years practicing this,
Now the synchronicities I don't miss...
It means being in my body, instead of mind,
Or the divine path I will not find...

Divine Unfolding

Today a new chapter will begin,
Because I've been following the signs within...
When I tune in, I am so connected,
And through life I'm easily directed...
All I have to do is come back to trust,
As I always say, the trust is a must...
And to trust you must know thyself,
And not be swayed by everyone else...
Because this is your life, you can decide,
From your vibration, you cannot hide...
As your outer vision, will reflect what's in,
Do your inner work, so freedom can begin...
Because, when you clear out the old,
Your divinely aligned life, will unfold...

{ 98 }

Reflection Of You

Life will always show you where you're at,
You'll be shown by what you attract...
And maybe it will seem easier to blame the external,
But know, it's a reflection of your internal...
So how can you shift your vibration,
It's realising that you're always in creation...
So what is it that you're creating,
Do you see a pattern in those you're dating...
If so, ask, where am I coming from lack,
Is it to myself, I am not giving back...
Because if you are not trusting yourself,
You're not going to be able to trust anyone else...
And if you are not loving yourself,
You're not going to feel love from anyone else...
It really is so simple to see,
If you ask, what is this mirror teaching me...
If you are seeking divine union,
Know that loving yourself, is the ultimate reunion...
If you aren't able to choose yourself,
You will never fully be chosen by someone else...

{ 99 }

Sweet Spot Within

It's always about the journey along the way,
When you live in the present moment each day...
Because nothing else exists apart from now,
You are constantly creating from here somehow...
If you don't like what you currently see,
You'll need to take more time to just be...
Finding that sweet spot within,
Where you feel your cells sing...
Life creates from this place,
And it will arrive in the 3D space...
You are the creator of your reality,
And we live in a world of duality...
So in every moment you have a decision to make,
Is it the flow or struggle option you will take...
One thought at a time creating your dream,
You choose if it's challenging or serene...
When you know how you desire to feel,
You'll be able to trust what the subtleties reveal...

{ 100 }

Expectation & Boundaries

I felt her energy, with not a word,
What she was thinking, had been heard...
I reached out to see if she was OK,
And I was left feeling free, at the end of the day...
She has never liked it when I choose myself,
Cause she wants my attention above everyone else...
But no longer do I abandon myself for another,
Not a friend, partner or a lover...
And I now call-in reflections of that,
One's that don't expect me to be their door mat...
See the areas where you aren't giving to yourself,
And expecting everything from everyone else...
I'd be doing you a disservice to pander to you,
Even though that's what you want me to do...
I'm no longer an energetic match for that,
And I won't take it personally as you attack...
Because I know these times can be tough,
And you may think my friendship isn't enough...
But I trust one day you'll eventually see,
That me honoring me, will help set you free...
But first you must look within instead of project,
Otherwise, you'll keep feeling feelings of reject...

Daily Alignment

I'm curious as to why I'm here,
I'm in alignment, that much is clear...
All the beautiful gifts of today,
The freedom to come what may...
The open road with no place to be,
Just time and space to truly see...
See the beauty that is here in the now,
It then attracts more beauty somehow...
And what is beauty if you cannot see,
Beauty is what I've created in my reality...
And maybe not all see what I do,
But what they see in their reality is true...
It's true to what they have created,
Even the parts they may have hated...
Because the more we focus on a thought,
Will determine what we are bought...
And energy flows where attention goes,
So be careful with those ebbs & flows...
It's easy to get dragged down by another,
But not if you are your own divine lover...
Because you would have realised the secret gift,
The gift that will help humanity uplift...

RACHEL HEANEY

It's keeping yourself in alignment each day,
And not being affected by what others may say...
People may call it selfish when you honour you,
But that is the most powerful thing you can do...
Because if your energy isn't a full yes to them,
They will one day thank you for that time when...
When you stayed true to the highest timeline,
Even if it meant to them, you no longer align...
Because you aren't here to people please,
The thought may actually make you wheeze...
So my greatest advice for you,
And a suggestion on what you could do...
It's stay true to yourself each day,
And you'll feel relief in every way...
Doors will open out of the blue,
When you trust the divine compass inside of you...

{ 102 }

Flames

Like a candle burning bright,
Two flames can light up the night...
One standing strong keeping the wick up right,
The other melting into a liquid sight...
Where they both dance & mirror each other,
You could call them the ultimate lover...
Coming together in unison to play their part,
To create this expansive love art...
Expansive in the ways it lights up the night,
It illuminates what we may want hidden from sight...
But the flame will burn away what serves you no more,
So yourself reflected in another, you will then adore...
Some may try to dim your light,
Because it's shining way too bright...
And for those who enjoy sitting in the dark,
May not want to be lit by your spark...
But they can close their eyes and not see,
That your flame will set them free...
It will melt them into surrendered bliss,
Then it's your light they will really miss...

{ 103 }

Tuned In

Being tuned in is the greatest feeling,
Connected to all life and what it's revealing...
It will let you know if you're off track,
Because your joy & satisfaction will start to lack...
But one step at a time you can realign,
When you tune back into the divine...
The divine is within, in every way,
Answering your vibration every day...
So start with being grateful for one thing now,
And see how more gratitude will find you somehow...
The more you notice, the more you receive,
Some may find this hard to believe...
But give it a try, there's so much to gain,
And your doubts will soon, no longer remain...
Because you've started trusting within,
Now the best chapter of your life can begin...

{ 104 }

The Calling Of This Book

I can feel the calling of my next book,
It will be a guide through all it took...
To live this life of full flow,
Where I'm guided easily where to go...
Different ways to guide you into alignment,
Where you choose how your energy is spent...
Do you choose the same lesson on repeat,
Or do you choose synchronicities to meet...
The path of least resistance is the key,
Give it a try and you will see...
You get to choose the life you desire,
And my intention is that this book will inspire...
Showing those that feel the call to read,
From their old patterns they will be freed...
The law of attraction will help them find,
So this book they will effortlessly be aligned...

… { 105 }

Honour The Truth Inside

You know that feeling you've been trying to ignore,
But that feeling keeps coming more & more...
Illuminating what it is that needs to change,
And what inner patterns need to rearrange...
Yes, that thing, you know the one,
That feeling that makes you want to run...
Maybe there is something you need to communicate,
Where there is a truth, you get to state...
You may worry what speaking your truth will mean,
But trust me I know, it will be so very freeing...
You'll feel the relief wash over you,
When you honour the truth inside of you...

Change Your Thoughts

We all are the programmers for ourselves,
It's not actually up to anyone else...
Others will show you where you need to adjust,
Listening to your intuition is a must...
Because if you don't like what you are seeing,
Change your thoughts and it will be so freeing...
When you are vibrating so high,
Then the reflection will not lie...
It will reward you for your progress,
And it won't mean going into another process...
Because sometimes they may keep you stuck,
Where you will think you are out of luck...
Be ok with this moment now,
And you'll see it improve somehow...

{ 107 }

Seeking

When you notice another seeking,
What is it that they are needing...
Is it to seek love from another,
Rather than being their internal lover...
They struggle to be on their own,
As their mind often likes to roam...
Creating stories that they're not enough,
Sitting in their own company can be tough...
Maybe you try to save this type,
Because being a people pleaser is your vibe...
If you could distract them from their pain,
You'd think you're a hero when their pain wouldn't remain...
Yet you now see you were only holding them back,
Your people pleasing was keeping them off track...
And there is no track if you're not being yourself,
And you're taking advice from everyone else...
Only you know what to do,
If you want to live what is true...

{ 108 }

Exploring

The Daintree keeps calling me back,
When I listen, I'm on the right track...
Guided to those I'm meant to meet,
With the Earth beneath my bare feet...
Connected to all that is here for me,
So much beauty I constantly see...
Feeling the energy wash over my being,
I'm in full flow and it's so very freeing...
My favourite feeling is right now,
Where everything else fades away somehow...
My senses tune into this sacred space,
And suddenly I'm filled with grace...
The sand beneath my feet holding me,
The beautiful sunset I get to see...
Hearing the birds chatting in the trees,
Feeling the bliss of the gently breeze...
The knowing that I'm right where I'm meant to be,
Because I trusted the whispers that guided me...

Clarity

Clarity is found by the choices we make,
There will be things we want to give & take...
Refining to get clearer on what you desire,
Things that bring discomfort will help to inspire...
Because when you can determine what you dislike,
You will then know how to call in more of what you do like...
And life is full of expansion & ease,
Once aligned, life will give you what you please...
If you think that life is a chore,
It will give you more and more...
But if you see and feel life as bliss,
Life will give you more you cannot miss...
So take a minute so you can see,
What life's like to feel so free...

Back To Your Heart

When reached within, it's then unlocked,
It's you, that would have kept it blocked...
If you were seeking the external first,
Divine union would have been a constant thirst...
When you find the key inside your heart,
It's when you'll create the greatest art...
So follow the threads back to your heart,
It is the guidance you need from the start...
Let go of fear, all that exists is love,
You've been bought here, from above...
Creating all that you desire,
Living a life that can truly inspire...
So may you trust and follow what's true,
And experience all the love, you came here to...

{ 111 }

Divinely Aligned

He appeared to me, out of the blue,
And at that first glance, I instantly knew...
I knew I'd been guided to him,
I felt all the tingles within...
In a world where no one existed,
It was him, I no longer resisted...
I could feel his energy, and had done for a while,
It was a soul recognition, from that first smile...
So much happening with no words spoken,
Our divine union, had been awoken...
Awoken in this 3D reality,
Where we could feel the polarity...
He honours me, like no one I've ever met,
I knew him, when we hadn't met yet...
Because he is me, and I am him,
We reflect the love back, from within...
We both found our way back home,
Because into the depths, we did roam...
Finding our big, beautiful heart,
Which had been guiding us, from the start...

Humble Men

I love men so extremely much,
For everything they do & every little touch...
They have been taught to hold it all together,
And that conditioning may last forever...
But I want these men to know I see them,
And that their feelings they can befriend...
All they have done to hold strong,
I know their path was never wrong...
But now I get to see them for what they've done,
And all the trials and tribulations they've overcome...
It brings tears of gratitude to my eyes,
Their courage and humbleness not in disguise...
Because I see them for who they are,
Even though they may carry a past scar...
I want them to know it's safe to feel,
Their human self is safe to reveal...
I'll hold that safe space,
So they feel unconditional loves embrace...

Dream Spell

We must dedicate to ourselves,
Before we can nurture anyone else...
Otherwise, we are giving from lack,
And then more lack, we will attract...
Take time to be in your own energy field,
A solid foundation within, you will build...
You will realise the true gift of being,
Connected to self, is so very freeing...
You'll realise you've yearned for it since birth,
It's been your journey, while here on Earth...
When you operate from a space of cooperation,
You'll see life as your own creation...
Guided to spaces that light you up,
The energy easily fills your cup...

Remembering The Love

Trust the wave you came in on,
Remembering the love, from where you came from...
You journey through life, learning to communicate,
Learning it's from your heart, where you create...
When you connect to your breath, in a conscious way,
You'll hear what the heart, has to say...
Transcending the limiting beliefs of the mind,
Because in your heart, pure love, you will find...
Connecting you to spirit in this moment now,
Creating a death of the ego, if you allow...
You will then realise the power in this,
As you feel connected to pure bliss...

{ 115 }

Unification

Coming into unity creates a bigger dream,
Some may ask "what does that mean"...
It means the intention of two is amplified,
And will manifest all you've desired...
Attracting it all through your intuition,
You'll notice as it comes into fruition...
Allowing abundance to flow with ease,
As you lap up the sun and cool breeze...
You become so magnetic when aligned,
Living on purpose, miracles you'll find...
You're so powerful when you trust that feeling,
Being present to all the gifts it is revealing...

Polarity

Our polarity is the target they need,
So the heart activation can be freed...
Finding stability amongst the storm,
May be your current norm...
As you pave the way back home,
Through polarity shifts you'll need to roam...
Awareness of the subtle feelings,
And the hearts revealing's...
Knowing your intuition is flowing more,
Life offers so much for you to adore...
Challenges may come your way,
But it's how you handle them each day...
Guided by a higher intelligence, you thrive,
Entering the galactic portal, to feel alive...

{ 117 }

Heart Based Reality

When you activate your vision to survive,
Is when your soul mission will come alive...
Uniting with your internal instinct,
Will stop humanity becoming extinct...
So allow your life force to flow,
So future light tribes will grow...
Part of your gift and service to humanity,
Is creating a heart-based reality...
When you're guided from the heart space,
Like water, you'll flow with ease and grace...
Creating a massive ripple effect,
It's your heart space you need to protect...
Allowing multiple heart connections each day,
And following what the heart has to say...

Peace On Earth

Earth is in a state of rebalance,
And a deep state of remembrance...
Balancing out the planetary grid,
From all that karma did...
Karma from the past as people tried to control,
Their karmic load has now taken its toll...
Illuminating the darkness with light,
So they can't keep hidden from sight...
They now have a choice to evolve,
The mind control they will need to solve...
Not allowing the mind to take them from their heart,
Journeying to the heart was the mission from the start...
So please take this opportunity to see,
That you're a reflection of me...
And we all have our roles to play,
To bring peace on Earth each day...
Let the old versions of self die,
Allowing grief and any tears to cry...
Yourself is all you ever need,
To allow past patterning's to be freed...
Guided by spirit every single day,
When you listen to what the heart has to say...

{ 119 }

Rhythmic Life

Life works as a rhythm of art,
And gets better when living from the heart...
Beauty radiates from within,
And a glowing radiance it will bring...
Reflected back in what you see,
The elegance of life when you just be...
So are you creating from a balanced space,
Do you allow yourself to move with ease and grace...
When you take time to truly go within,
Your power will be doubled and start to sing...

{ 120 }

Harmonize

When we harmonize within ourselves,
It's easy to love everyone else...
Loyalty to self then ripples out,
And that is what soul connection is about...
The process to get back to the heart,
Is in the beingness and life as art...
Staying in integrity every day,
Allowing your hearts truth to guide the way...
Where time is never ending,
And consciousness is ascending...
Create from that place,
And life will be filled with grace...

The Innocent Gift

How often do you allow yourself to play,
Take this as a sign you need to do it today...
Allowing the innocent child within to sing,
And noticing all the laughter and joy it will bring...
Noticing how much of life is an illusion,
And has created way too much confusion...
So stop and see the magic that kids see,
They know how to live a life so free...
Set your intention for more magic today,
And see what accomplishments come your way...

Disconnect To Reconnect

They got smarter and smarter, and we fell into the trap,
Addicted to our phones, our energy started to lack...
Some may say, they are all we need,
Then another new version, they soon breed...
With more features, and apps to keep us addicted,
Before long, life without a phone, seems restricted...
Voice noting, photo shooting, searching and scrolling,
Oblivious to the addiction trap, that's unfolding...
I had fallen deep into this trap too,
Then some guidance, came out of the blue...
It was time to spend less time on my phone,
Out in nature, the best phone free zone...
Exploring this beautiful planet, we live on,
Connecting to nature, where nothing feels wrong...
Everything becomes so clear,
Whenever my phone is not near...
I feel so peaceful and connected to all that is,
And the beauty of each day, I cannot miss...
Spending more time offline,
Has been so incredibly divine...
The times that I come back online,
I get a headache and I don't feel fine...

RACHEL HEANEY

I didn't realise the effect, it had on me each day,
Until I spent more, and more time away...
So now I enjoy less screen time,
And to more blessing I do align...
I felt guided to share this poem with you,
In case you're guided to do a phone detox too...

Your Own Whispers

Today I switched into another gear,
I took steps of action for my career...
So I can support people in many ways,
And fulfil my soul mission for the rest of my days...
Dedicating to myself, I then enchant,
Releasing the ego, as I chant...
Remembering I am nothing & everything,
And it's through the subtleties that bring...
Synchronicity as I follow my path,
Not hiding in fear behind a mask...
As I like to share what comes through,
In case it's also a message for you...
And who would I be if I didn't share my gift,
When it's here to help the consciousness uplift...
So I'm reminded to do what is guided,
So the consciousness is not divided...
We all have a role to play,
Just trust your own whispers each day...
Don't be swayed by another voice,
As you have your own free will and choice...

Dedicated To Be

Can you stay dedicated to be right here,
Where all thought patterns disappear...
There will be no need, for anything else,
When you tune into now, and yourself...
Letting go of all you think you have to do,
Because your greatest gift, is when you be you...
Your truest, most authentic version is your gift,
Being true to you, will help the consciousness shift...
There is no pressure to get things done,
Because when you're stressed, you're not having fun...
And creation holds a vibration that will live on,
So your joy and pleasure, sure do belong...
As more of that, is needed right now,
So let pleasure inspire you somehow...
Pleasure and joy come in many ways,
It's the things that brighten up your days...
So do more of what lights you up,
More of the things that fill your cup...
Life will reward you along the way,
When you include more fun and play...

{ 125 }

A True Gift

Time in my own company and space,
All the creativity & visions I embrace...
Guiding me how I can best serve humanity,
Using my own unique gifts & creativity...
Another book to be shared far and wide,
So people can use it as a guide...
To help and support them on their way,
Helping them to listen to the soul whispers each day...
Sometimes the whispers won't make sense to the mind,
But when followed, a true gift you will find...
And not just a gift for yourself,
It's also a gift for everyone else...

Divinely Aligned Mirror

Can you see your reflection in another,
Do they reflect back your inner lover...
That will depend if you're in your heart,
The ego mind has wanted control from the start...
But this journey of life is a walk back home,
Through the mind control madness you will need to roam...
You can't bypass the things that hold you back,
Or the vital wisdom you will always lack...
You can't advance in consciousness if you ignore the truth,
The one they've tried to hide since your youth...
But this is the life you came to breakthrough,
Trusting yourself, you know what you have to do...
If you can't trust yourself, you'll become a slave to the system,
But as you start trusting thyself, you'll gain more wisdom...
So there is a choice you'll need to make,
You get to choose which adventure you take...
One full of growth and reward,
Or one of control and discord...
Neither choice is wrong or right,
You'll just experience a different reality each day and night...
May you have the courage to stay true to you,
You deep down know what you've got to do...

Social Anxiety

Social anxiety is more common than you know,
And can really take people out of their flow...
Faced with someone that is new,
They may not know what to do...
Or maybe they're not in a familiar place,
So they feel awkward, and on edge in the space...
It's hard to chat about random things,
They may love using the distraction, that a dog brings...
They may feel more connected to pets and trees,
As they take anxiety away with a swift breeze...
Maybe they used to numb anxiety with drinking,
And now wonder what they were thinking...
Abusing their body just to go out,
That's what their social anxiety was about...
The other option was to stay home alone,
Where their inner demons they'd have to roam...
Now they love their own time and space,
Being alone, they are filled with grace...

The Truth You Will Find

Do you take time out for stillness in your day,
Where your ego mind will fall away...
Allowing you to be in the space of nothingness,
Where your mind gets to experience emptiness...
When you remember you're all & nothing at the same time,
This remembrance can be so beautifully divine...
There is no questioning in that space,
You're just filled with the voids embrace...
Floating, and in an infinite place of peace,
Where all your thoughts will easily cease...
What a beautiful place to be,
Then even more beauty you will see...
As you've created that space within,
So much peace it will then bring...
The more and more time you do this,
The truth you will not be able to miss...
And the truth can't be found in the logical mind,
Go into stillness and the truth you will find...

{ 129 }

Nurtured By He

Today I got beautifully nurtured by him,
I love the presence & connection he can bring...
His connection through every touch,
I simply adore this man so much...
He is teaching me and helping me to grow,
There is so much I didn't know...
He is teaching me through the heart,
Guiding me back to the very start...
Where we are life experiencing ourselves,
And have to be discerning of everyone else...
Seeing ourselves reflected as the Earth,
To help in Mumma Gaia's rebirth...
He nurtured me like I was the mother,
And treated me like no other...
What a gift this man is to me,
He is helping me to even more clearly see...

{ 130 }

The Key To All You Crave

What is the message that wants to come through,
Is it a message for me or for you...
I use writing as a way to access,
The universal mind it brings success...
Success on this journey back home,
Where repeated dark paths, we don't have to roam...
Life is actually incredibly simple when we just be,
We see how much is an illusion, in this reality...
Connected to the eternal within,
A peaceful satisfaction it will bring...
The void is the most delicious space,
And is the key to all you crave...
Or everything you thought you craved,
Creating from how your vibration has behaved...
So is there something that needs clearing up,
Before you'll feel that abundance and luck...

Gifts Of Life

Mumma Earth gave us all we need,
But so many got lost in greed...
Instead of sharing the gifts around,
And respecting what was given from the ground...
People created foods that were dead of life,
Made with chemicals which put our health in strife...
People got so lost in making more money to fulfil themselves,
They didn't care about the health or wellbeing of anyone else...
It's such a sad thing to see,
People are unable to just be...
They are missing the beauty in each day,
And they aren't connected to what their heart has to say...
Because if they were, they'd realise they've lived a lie,
They were programmed and fell into the trap, they cannot deny...
May they find compassion within,
And allow their heart awakening to begin...
Where everything that isn't from a place of love, must go,
And to each next step, they will then easily flow...
They will remember that feeling,
And it will be so incredibly healing...
They will meet like-minded souls,
Who have also given up control...

{ 132 }

The Compass Inside Of You

What works for some, won't work for another,
So we must never judge or mislead each other...
We all have our unique paths to take,
And there will be many choices to make...
We may need to take a tougher path,
Because there may be a truth to unmask...
And without knowing what doesn't feel right,
We may lose our third eye vision or sight...
The message that always comes through,
Is that you must trust the guidance inside of you...
Because everyone else's advice comes from their filtered view,
They can never know the compass that is inside of you...
So you must be discerning who you trust,
Listening to your inner guidance is a must...
Never has there been a more important time to choose you,
To have faith and trust the wisdom within, on what to do...
This may be tough at first,
But soon you'll quench your thirst...
The thirst to live the eternal life,
The one where there is no strife...

Out-Dated Beliefs

In this moon of challenge, I feel the motions,
The energy clearing out stagnant emotions…
Releasing any outdated beliefs,
So I can return to inner peace…
Manifesting the reality in tune with the divine,
Where beautiful reflections, I do align…
Perfecting my discipline of what I'm creating,
Then aligned intentions I am stating…
To be, and act from my core as love,
That message always getting clearer from above…
My body is my vessel, and I must treat it with respect,
Or certain thoughts and feelings it will try to eject…
Using my life force to rid the old,
Letting go of old conditioning I had been told…
There is no one coming to save us from here,
It's our own responsibility, to choose love over fear…
Remembering who we are at our core,
Feeling that peace within, we don't need anymore…
Allowing the senses to stir up through your spine,
Through your body, you can connect to the divine…

Outside The Box

Have you ever thought 'outside the box',
Where the truth easily unlocks...
The box being the television,
Which equates to the 'tell lie vision'...
The things you see and hear on there,
Are not coming from a place of care...
It's been designed to keep you trapped,
Where a life of fear you can easily attract...
When you're in a state of fear,
It's when your connection to self will disappear...
The self is so much more than we were taught,
And many conditionings that lie has bought...
We are more powerful than we may know,
Finding stillness within is where we need to go...
Then finding the source within,
That is where unity consciousness can begin...
Remembering the truth at our core,
There won't be a need to strive for more...
If you're being guided to search outside yourself,
You've been misled by someone else...
Try creating stillness within,
And you'll feel the peace it will bring...

Have The Courage

Where is all your time being spent,
Where is your mind paying the most rent...
I say mind because these days there is so much mind control taking place,
Just stop and take a look around in the common space...
People are addicted to screens that are keeping them trapped,
Not trusting their inner wisdom that is perfectly mapped...
There is currently a war against the mind,
While being mind controlled, peace, you will not find...
Like a frog being slowly cooked up in a pot,
You don't realise what's good for you, and what is not...
Until you jump out of the pot and feel your natural state,
Stop allowing those controlling the pot, to dictate your fate...
Have the courage to set yourself free,
Take that leap, and you will see...
You'll see the underlying fire they had beneath you,
And realise they never wanted you to see what's true...

Your Internal Map

The synchronicities will keep you on track,
They are the signposts for your internal map…
Notice them and the signs they bring,
And know you're following your alignment within…
The more synchronicities that you see,
Know they are guiding you, to set you free…
Free from the old, outdated belief,
When connected within, life is so sweet…
I call it being divinely aligned,
It's when you're not stuck, in your mind…
You've found another piece of your map,
And your inner being is happy about that…
As another piece found means you're closer to the truth,
Mind you, this is not the same puzzle from your youth…
You may spend a lifetime searching around,
But when you stop searching, it's easy to be found…
Sounds kind of ironic, I know,
But when you surrender, you'll easily flow…
You'll flow to the people, places or things,
And receive the puzzle piece it brings…
I'll give a little clue to you,
A piece is the peace, that is true…

The Program, Programming You

Is there a favorite program you like to watch on the TV,
If so, do you ask "what is this programming within me"...
As you sit on the couch, watching in a relaxed state,
You are the programmer's perfect type of bait...
You are in an alpha brain wave state, as you relax,
The perfect way they can brain wash you, about the vax...
Without you consciously knowing, what is taking place,
They have been able to hypnotise you, in your own space...
Do you notice how you feel after watching the news,
Your inner knowing, they will easily confuse...
Making you fear due to the stories they share,
Ask yourself, do they actually even care...
And are the stories they share even true,
Or are they just another program, programming you...
It's good to take a break from TV and see,
Spend time in nature, and you'll feel so free...
You'll realise it's kept you trapped in the box,
And you'll know you need a TV detox...

{ 138 }

Labels & Identities

Do you notice yourself identifying with the ego mind,
Needing a label of who you are, which you'll never find...
As you're not what you do, or the label someone may give you,
Your ego's need for more, will stop you living so true...
Your mind might be scattered, and all over the place,
Acting like finding new labels, is some sort of race...
And maybe it is in your reality,
And what even is normality...
There are people selling courses, everywhere you look,
So the ego's mind, they can easily hook...
Because if the ego thinks it can be better than someone else,
Then it will continue to seek outside of itself...
Not realising, it is whole within,
So the peace, it will never bring...

{ 139 }

The Earth's Crystal Core

Today I felt so guided to give back,
It's a continuous journey with no lack...
I did a blessing on the waters within and without,
And was shown what my massive crystal collection was about...
I'd been gathering crystals for many years,
And the joy they've provided has bought me to tears...
But I realise they don't actually belong to me,
I sent them back to the Earth where they can truly be...
The Earth has been missing the pieces of her heart,
So giving back her crystals is a good start...
I'll release them back as per divine guidance each day,
And I'll trust what the whispers say...
It felt so good to return them in the sacred place,
I then felt the divine move me with grace...

{ 140 }

Free Will

Currently you still have free will,
But if you comply, your freedom will be nil...
The plan has been unfolding for a while,
And some have seen it coming from a mile...
They have tried to warn you before it's too late,
Before they have full control to dictate your fate...
It may have been easier to turn a blind eye,
It's a lot to know the truth, I cannot deny...
When you realise they have never cared about your health,
They have just been taken over by greed and wealth...
But what is money when you don't have happiness,
You'll be trapped in a controlled sense of loneliness...
Always been taught to believe you need more,
A bigger home, a new phone or more things to adore...
This is the trap they want you to fall in,
No true peace or happiness it will bring...
Before too long you'll be wanting more again,
I invite you to stop and think back to a time when...
When you felt content and peace within yourself,
When you weren't feeling restricted or controlled by anyone else...
Maybe you hadn't noticed the restrictions and laws that have
gradually been put in place,

Divinely Aligned

And how you are being watched and tracked when in your own private space...
Every word that you speak and emotion you feel,
Is been recorded by AI, and so much about you it can reveal...
And as for the injections they forced onto you,
I won't even start on what that now enables them to do...
This isn't meant to inflict more fear on you,
It's just to illuminate some things that may ring true...
Allowing you to have an open mind to another point of view,
So you can know in yourself what really feels true...
You may feel there is no way out,
You've been told many lies I have no doubt...
Please think about the children and future generations to come,
Without us making a change, humanity will be done...
We can all help in our own individual way,
Maybe you can just set your intention each day...
Request that any harm that's been sent your way,
Be sent back to its rightful owners each day...
So then they can finally see,
What they've been doing to humanity...
May they all come back to a place of love,
Which was always the mission sent from above...

Stillness & Art

As I sit here under my favorite trees,
I feel the delightful cool breeze...
Listening to the waves gently kiss the shore,
I don't feel the need for anymore...
The sun shining down creating patterns on the sand,
I love the ancient wisdom I receive from this land...
When you bring your life back into simplicity,
You will have more time to express your creativity...
And creativity comes when present in the now,
Connected to everything and nothing somehow...
So create more stillness and more art,
Creativity is what birthed anything from the start...
So what wants to move through you,
Can you find stillness allowing it to...

{ 142 }

Offering Of Gratitude

Can you allow gratitude to rise within you,
Where there is no forcing you need to do...
It just naturally comes up as you offer it as an energetic gift,
It is a blessing to receive as you feel your consciousness uplift...
You can't be conscious if you don't notice the beauty around you,
It's endless, and will send life force energy through you...
It's a beautiful energy exchange with Mumma Earth,
She's been constantly offering it to you since your birth...
Maybe you weren't always giving the blessing of gratitude back,
So the gift of beauty you didn't attract...
It was always there trying to get your attention,
But maybe your focus was looking in the wrong direction...
So be more present in the now,
And you'll have more moments of wow...

… { 143 }

Out Of The Blue

Have you been present enough, when you meet someone new,
To listen beyond the words, to the wisdom they share with you…
It may be subtle in the words they say,
Or it may be how they be true to themselves every day…
Noticing the old beliefs that may appear,
Seeing the reflection of where you may still fear…
Knowing that there are gifts for us wherever we go,
Wisdom in the energy we are ready to know…
Always ask life to provide the next step for you,
And be ready as a form of guidance will come out of the blue…

Here To Create

Like a figure eight,
We are here to create...
What goes around comes around,
So be sure to keep two feet on the ground...
Reminding you of your connection,
Letting life force guide your direction...
In every moment there is time to create,
What you choose will dictate your fate...
So if you are ignoring your inner call,
From divine alignment you will soon fall...
Take action from a grounded place,
If the mind is busy, create the space...
Allowing clear guidance, to come through,
On what it is, you're next to do...
If you keep ignoring the call,
Your energy will lack, more and more...
So what is it you're being asked to do,
To that inner voice call, you must stay true...

Animal Guidance

Day of the eagle, where I'm guided with such ease,
Flowing through my day, like a beautiful spring breeze...
Bringing the formless, into form,
Creating my own unique day, is my norm...
Greeted by many creatures, along the way,
First it was a cassowary, saying 'good day'...
They use their heads, in matters of the heart,
Probably what I've also done, from the start...
They also like to remain invisible, to most human beings,
So it's a beautiful reflection of me, I was seeing...
I saw two black cockatoos, as I felt I'd be in The Daintree to stay,
They're a sign of liberation, confirming I was going the right way...
It felt good, and ultra-clear,
I know I'm guided, when they are near...
A dingo was also, on the side of the road,
A sign of having a guardian, in full protection mode...
They are known to keep evil spirits away,
So they are welcomed on the land, each day...
Then there was a big croc, as I crossed back on the barge,
It wasn't hiding, and it was so very large...
Ancient protectors, of this land,
The more I'm here, the more I understand...

Principles & Guides

These are the seven principles, and my guide,
I live in full flow, when this wisdom, I abide...
Ike; the world is what we think it is, so be aware,
Our thoughts create our reality, so take ultra-care...
Kala; there are no limits to what you desire,
So dream big, and you will then truly inspire...
Makia; energy flows where attention goes,
So be intentional, on where it effortlessly flows...
Manawa; now is the moment of all that is,
So be present, and you will feel more bliss...
Mana; all power comes from within,
So tuning into self, is where to begin...
Aloha; to love is to be happy, that much I know,
So make sure to spread love, wherever you go...
Pono; effectiveness is the measure of truth,
Follow the path of least resistance, and share it with the youth...
May this poem act as a reminder today,
So you'll have more flow, and ease come your way...

Magical Orchestration

Do you set your intention to create,
Or do you just leave it up to fate...
When I set my intention and then let it be,
Life magically orchestrates things for me...
It's such a blessing to see how it all falls into place,
It happens when you create stillness and space...
You are not needing your manifestation to come to fruition,
You're just living day by day, following your intuition...

The Gift Of Rain

Thank you for bringing the rain,
At times I didn't want it to remain...
But I now see even clearer the gift,
And how it helps the consciousness uplift...
Giving the rainforest it's vibrant green,
So the summer days can feel so serene...
It's also watering the plants so they can grow,
And also allow the creeks to effortlessly flow...
Giving us fresh water to drink,
And a place where we don't have to think...
Because the water cleanses away what serves us no more,
And helps grow abundantly delicious food for us to adore...
After the rain the sun will come out,
And you'll see even more beauty about...
May you treasure the gift of rain as it fills your water tanks,
Filling you with gratitude and blessings as you give your thanks...

Self-Generate Energy

Some days you won't feel like doing a thing,
Take rest on those days to feel the nourishment from within...
But if there is too much time of rest,
New energy you will not be able to digest...
You will need to self-generate by taking action,
You'll soon feel energized, it's the law of attraction...
The more energy you expend the more that will come back,
It might seem illogical and off the right track...
But give it a try and you will see,
You can self-generate energy so effortlessly...
Once you get started the energy will flow,
You'll have the momentum to go and go...

Divine Man

I now understand the meaning of the divine man,
He can sit in the stillness when no one else can...
He lets go of thoughts, and is present in the now,
He emanates bliss in the most magical way, somehow...
He doesn't get lost in distraction,
So to the divine woman, there is attraction...
Both knowing themselves as the eternal,
They know, to know thyself, is internal...
In body, as there is no other place to be,
They can reach the place, where thoughts are set free...
To meet another, who knows what is true,
Is such a gift that came out of the blue...
As I wasn't seeking, outside of myself,
I attracted someone whole, within themself...
Being together, is double the bliss,
And each moment, I feel grateful for this...

{ 151 }

The Truth

What if I said, the truth you won't find,
If you're searching for it, in your mind...
You won't even find it, through my word,
Because the truth I speak of, is unheard...
It's the vast space within yourself,
You won't find it from anyone else...
As it's you, who holds the key, to who you truly are,
You really don't even have to search very far...
In fact, stop searching altogether,
Be present as you observe the weather...
Then focus on your breath, as it enters you,
Focusing on your breath, is what you can start to do...
Then feel the sensations in your body, from your head to your toes,
Even noticing all the smells, that are entering your nose...
Knowing that everything is always happening within you,
The thoughts will try to come, and this is what you can do...
Acknowledge there is a thought, even when you try switch off the mind,
Even acknowledge, if you judge yourself for thinking, and more peace you will find...
Give it a try, and you'll start to see,
When you quieten the mind, you will feel so free...

Peace That Resides In You

There is a familiar peace, that resides within you,
When you find it, nothing else will feel more true...
It's the place of empty space, that births everything,
It births everything, from the stillness of nothing...
We spend most of our existence in this human form,
Trying to find that place of peace which was our norm...
The place to find it, is within,
Where your cells will start to sing...
Singing with delight as you've found your way home,
Realising it was through the mind, you didn't have to roam...
Because it's letting go of all thoughts, and imagination,
As you remember, you are the portal of creation...

Seeds Of Truth

We are like trees, birthed onto this Earth,
Like us, the trees go through birth...
They come from a seed, planted into the mother,
And are possibly protected, by another...
Allowing the correct nourishment from the ground,
Soon enough, through the soil, the sunlight they have found...
Being met by their father Sun,
And held by their Earthly Mum...
Growing their base, influenced by those who come into the space,
Is it a flower, or seed they will be here to gift from grace...
Each branch showing a new chapter of their existence,
They keep growing through any part of resistance...
Any seeds that they may sprout,
Will help release any of their doubt...
And as for the flowers that will grow,
It will illuminate their beauty, so they know...
That they are a gift on this Earth,
And are helping through this rebirth...
The leaves representing the impression they leave,
Allowing someone to see, and truly believe...
That life is always reflecting back our magnificence,
Nothing in your life, is of insignificance...

The Pain Body

Your pain body may get activated more some days,
It may try to steal your peace in many ways...
Old stories try to sabotage your progress,
Maybe in the past, you would have been a mess...
But this time you observe what is running rampant in your mind,
Knowing by surrendering and allowing, it the peace you will find...
But not allowing it to go into an unstable cycle,
Where the same thought patterns are on recycle...
You're now consciously allowing that story to go,
It's not the truth, you deep down know...
Because the truth is peace,
And in presence, it will increase...
You now don't judge yourself for still having this thought,
You now know it just stems from the things you were taught...

Life Force

It's a feeling that is always available to you,
Maybe you haven't been taught what you need to do...
If you can be present in your space,
You will soon be filled with grace...
Grace is the feeling you feel inside,
When it's presence you abide...
Allowing the thoughts of what you think to melt away,
All you have is this moment now, every single day...
So can you at least take a few moments of stillness to yourself,
I promise, you will benefit, as well as everyone else...
Observe any thoughts that try to enter,
And without judgement, just find your centre...
This is a practice, and will get easier along the way,
And you will feel more peace, in your day to day...

Godly Self

Have you been taught that God is someone outside yourself,
I'm here to remind you, you have direct access within thyself...
You are God, or the consciousness within,
You have all the wisdom to bring...
You have the ability to heal,
Within, you know what's real...
God is the life force running through you,
I wonder if you realise what is true...
They have hidden this knowledge for too long,
Teaching people it's heaven or hell where they belong...
There is no truth to searching outside of you,
Find the stillness within and you'll know what's true...

Truth Whispers

What to share and what to not,
Is it a reminder for those who forgot...
Or is it too much for the limited mind,
So the hidden truth they will not find...
But what if those who are ready to evolve,
Are so grateful for what they've been told...
Without you sharing with them the real news,
They may only have the controlled point of views...
And maybe that is limiting the collective in some way,
It's up to them, how they respond at the end of the day...
I don't share to implant more fear,
I share because truth whispers in my ear...
Maybe I plant a seed in you,
And when that seed sprouts, you'll know what to do...
The subtle truth, like a seed, will sprout through the darkness,
And for a moment, your reality may seem like a mess...
But trust the evolution of the seed,
Once through the darkness, more light will breed...
All igniting each other of the same truth within,
When connected to our inner essence, peace it will bring...
Humanity will have broken through,
Clearing the mind control, was what we had to do...

{ 158 }

Love Of Life

Love is what we feel inside ourselves,
It doesn't come from someone else...
However, you can share in moments with another,
Where you're both connected to your inner lover...
The inner lover is source, the divine,
When connected within, a mirror you will align...
They will reflect back so you can see your love in the form of someone else,
But you must always remember that connection is found within the self...
Our inner connection reflects in the outer reality we see,
So ask yourself if you are loving your outer reality...
If not, it's time to look more into your internal being,
Connect to the life force within, and life you will start seeing...

{ 159 }

A Divine Reflection

Guided so clearly to where we were to meet,
His smiling face I got to greet...
Knowing I had been guided to him,
But not knowing what was about to begin...
Surrendering as the energy had me melt,
His divine presence was easily felt...
One day at a time not getting caught in old ways,
We got to actually enjoy each other's company in the coming days...
And then the days turned into weeks,
And it was clear we both hear what the wind speaks...
Learning and growing with each other by our side,
Next to this man there is nothing I have to hide...
As he hears the energy that is spoken with no words at all,
And when I'm needing support, he hears the call...
He is a man of integrity and pure heart,
And he is a beautiful form of art...
Connected to the love within, he is guided by his inner knowing,
And his healing touch has my whole-body glowing...
I'd always known I'd meet him one day,
I just had to keep listening to what my inner being had to say...
I'd heard a couple of years back,

Divinely Aligned

"Let's meet at the tree", but I fell a little off track,
As I wasn't sure where I would find this tree,
Only realising now, he meant the 'Daintree'...
So here I am living life from the vison I saw,
And knowing I don't need any more...
I have been provided with the greatest gift,
A divine reflection to help with the consciousness shift...

{ 160 }

Bio Field Activation

We each have our own bio field,
When activated it is our best shield...
To stop us from being controlled by the elite,
The power we hold within, is so neat...
Each day we must connect, and activate our protection suit,
Some may disagree, and try to dispute...
But our minds and bodies are being taken over,
There is so much they don't want us to uncover...
Tune into your auric field each day,
What are the subtleties trying to say...
Trust that you hold the key within,
Less time on your smart phone is where to begin...
They trace and track your every feeling and thought,
They can access more than you've ever been taught...
So be careful where your energy is spent,
As they know, to who and where you went...

Transcending The Mind

The cosmic wizard endures in order to enchant today,
Listening to what true presence has to say...
Transcending the mind,
Receptivity you will find...
Entering the void of timelessness,
Where you're guided by endlessness...
Expansion from letting go,
Receiving what you need to know...
The next step in the human path,
Being present is the first task...

… { 162 }

Feeling Content Within

The best way to receive is through feeling,
Through the feeling of what you want, miracles start revealing…
The truth is that anything is possible to bring into form,
But holding the feeling within may not be your norm…
But if you can stay in the feeling and pure presence,
You'll receive all your desire because of your essence…
But you must let go of the clinging hold of lack,
Or your desire will be going down another track…
Stay with the feeling of contentment within,
Is how the magic of form will begin…
Because your inner will be reflected in your external reality,
Finding presence within is the best type of creativity…

Concrete Jungle

Going into town is quite the trip,
And I feel the energy change really quick...
From lush forests of creeks and trees,
Where I easily flow through the cool breeze...
To a concrete jungle with each corner a tower,
It's a full blown 5G EMF shower...
My head starts pounding and my eyes can't see,
I easily realise how bad 5G is for me...
I didn't realise until I got out of the pot,
What feels good for my body and what does not...
They are killing us with the majority unaware,
And maybe some turn a blind eye and don't even care...
Because finding a place where you can safely be,
Maybe not something available in your reality...
But when you know that you can choose,
If it's your health and wellbeing you don't want to lose...
Be sure to see what feels best for you,
Trapped in a concrete jungle with a 5G tower view,
Or live a life of natural beauty that you came here to...

New Level Of Shielding Needed

There is a certain level of shielding needed,
For all the EMF's that have been seeded...
Our brains are being fried,
I could feel it as I cried...
Tears from all the pain,
What could I do so it wouldn't remain...
I thought my phone on flight mode was enough,
But I've found out these frequencies are ultra-tough...
I'd wrapped it in protective shielding,
But the magnetic force wasn't yielding...
The best thing to do to protect yourself,
Spend less time around devices as they harm the self...
Get out into nature to ground each day,
And when around tech, wrap faraday cloth around your head some way...

… { 165 } …

Contraction & Expansion

After there is an opening of the heart,
Then there's a connection pulling you apart...
From being in open hearted bliss,
To wondering if it's you they would even miss...
Trying to observe the stories playing in your mind,
Realising there is no truth you can find...
The ego has a pain body that's hard to release,
If you try to fight it the suffering will increase...
So the most important thing you can do,
Is surrender knowing the story isn't true...
And if the expansion contracts you in another direction,
Know that it's a divinely guided course correction...
Everyone plays a divine part for you,
Look back on your past and you'll know it's true...
Life is always working out for you,
Guiding you to meet people out of the blue...
As long as you're staying true to the divine,
Even more magic you will always align...
So take a breath and trust,
Letting go of fear is a must...
As fear doesn't exist where there is love,
So always choose love is the message from above...

Karma Clearing

Karma is an energy that doesn't lie,
You can't hide from it, as much as you try...
If you have done harm sometime in your past,
You'll experience the same, so it will not last...
This is how we come back to oneness and unity,
It's experiencing both ends of the duality...
Once you have received your serving of karma,
It's when you'll truly know your dharma...
So treat others how you would treat yourself,
You'll then get a mirrored version from someone else...
Then you will know what true unconditional love involves,
It may be different from what you'd been told...
It's when you've let go of judgement for yourself,
And you've journeyed through the karma from everyone else...
And now you know everyone has their own journey to take,
And you can love them even with the mistakes they make...

Synchronistic Feeling

It is the whisper of the divine,
Showing you that to the truth you align...
For it's in the truth there is flow,
Easily guided where to go...
Not trying to swim upstream,
That is not the way to the life you dream...
It comes in the surrendering and letting go,
Let go of fear, and go with the water flow...
As water doesn't have any blocks,
More openings and beauty easily unlocks...
Notice the divine gifts that come your way,
And the synchronicity in your day to day...
You'll be pleasantly surprised when in full flow,
Things easily unfold, and your mind will blow...
It is my greatest feeling,
I love the magic that is revealing...

New Level Of Sensitivity

I've become more sensitive to the energy at play,
And how it affects me each and every day...
Being on my phone or around 5G or WIFI,
I can feel my brain as it starts to fry...
When the powers at be turn up the dial,
I can feel it coming from a mile...
It's not natural and is horrendous for our health,
All because they want more power and wealth...
I thought I was sensitive to energy before,
But the intensity is getting more and more...
And since I've been spending time offline,
I feel every subtlety that isn't fine...
For the people that never take time away,
They don't know the harm that's coming their way...
It's a blessing and a curse to be a sensitive soul,
As you can feel all the ways they are trying to control...

Road Trip Back To Oneness

It's been many months since I set off on the road,
When I surrendered into full trust mode...
Where I knew something was guiding me,
And the next step was a map within me...
One I had been searching to find,
But it was not ever found in the mind...
It was about letting go of thought,
Many blessings that certainly bought...
It was about the subtle feeling,
And listening to what it was revealing...
It knew I would find the pieces of the map,
When in flow they easily fell into my lap...
Day by day as I pieced together the signs,
I was constantly amazed by what I aligned...
Then after nine days being guided by the,
It was him, in person, I got to see...
My soul instantly knew when our eyes met,
But I had no idea of the complete reason yet...
It became obvious when my plan to leave easily changed,
Because I was surrendering as things rearranged...
Effortlessly this beautiful connection came to be,
He is the most divine reflection of me...

RACHEL HEANEY

I've been inspired by him in so many ways,
And I'll feel love & gratitude for him for all my days...
Living together on the most sacred land,
I feel blessed beyond what most can understand...
We help each other to grow so much,
And we both love to support through touch...
He is a blessing that I treasure with my heart,
He is also inspiring my poetry art...

Pleasure Of Simplicity

We have a choice what is good for our being,
And when we choose our truth, it is so freeing...
But so many think it's not possible to be free,
They have been trapped in the mind slavery...
Not realising most of what they've been taught is a lie,
Once they surrender their egos, the truth they can't deny...
They then start flowing with such ease,
Feeling the subtlety of the gentle breeze...
Realising the pleasure of simplicity,
They start seeing blessings in their reality...
Everything changing for the better in a blink of an eye,
Things manifest so magically when they don't even try...

Floating Beauty

Magical days, enjoyed in many ways,
Submersed in nature, as the butterfly plays...
Flying free through the trees,
Effortlessly flowing in the breeze...
Bringing beauty to those that see,
They see the reflection of living so free...
Bright blue shimmering swimming hole,
Spending more time at this creek is my goal...
Sacred land holding me,
Nature's beauty I clearly see...
Floating around like in the mother's womb,
My first visit here didn't come too soon...

{ 172 }

The Most Rewarding Gift

To be of service is the most rewarding gift,
Not only to us, but to the others we uplift...
What would life be if no one was giving,
It would be a dis-service to what we call living...
So many don't know what it is to truly live,
If they did, they'd have a full cup to give...
Everyone is all part of the same energy pool,
But some think those that give, are a fool...
But they are giving from an overflowing cup,
So they can easily fill others up...
But those others must be open to receive,
Or the true gift of giving, they won't retrieve...
May the gift of giving spread far & wide,
Being of service doesn't mean you swallow your pride...

{ 173 }

Ocean Of Love

When we activate that loving feeling,
It is so very deeply healing...
Bonding together in loyalty,
You'll feel like you are royalty...
But not in a way you look down on everyone else,
When love is your compass, you're no better than anyone else...
You allow the love you feel within,
To allow the ripple of love to begin...
Soon enough, waves are flowing in every direction,
And everyone gets to feel the love and affection...
Reminding them they are but a drop in this ocean of love,
May all humans remember this, is the message from above...

… { 174 }

Heightened Senses

I have a heightened sense within,
It shows me where to begin...
If something feels not quite right,
My internal compass shines a light...
Pointing me in the right direction,
Taking me on a course correction...
I may not know why at the time,
But know I'm guided by the divine...
So I trust where I am being sent,
Today it was to the roof top tent...
Someone had stolen the cover from the shed,
I wondered if they're using it as a bed...
The other day I felt someone around,
Now today, the proof was found...

She Is Nature

She connects her bare feet to the ground,
And she feels the nature all around...
She feels the wind asking her to dance,
She knows she'd always take the chance...
Allowing herself to flow with such ease,
As she is caressed by the refreshing breeze...
The ancient trees whispering wisdom in her ear,
Saying, when surrounded by nature, there is nothing to fear...
Nature provides us with so much bliss,
A daily dose, she cannot miss...
Noticing how she feels in nature's embrace,
It's never an approval she has to chase...
Because nature has always loved us all unconditionally,
And she reflects that love so beautifully...

{ 176 }

Heavenly Existence

There is a heavenly place, and it's here,
When we choose love over fear...
Heaven will then easily appear,
The love within you will cheer...
Beauty in every sight you see,
You'll be filled with bubbles of glee...
You'll laugh at the craziness of living any other way,
And you will be rewarded and supported every day...
Thank the creator of all that is,
And you will feel more bliss...
Know that you are protected and provided for,
Just ask for assistance if you're ever needing more...

Natural High

Waking up early ready to go,
But to where, I did not know...
He suggested a bike ride down to the swimming hole,
So I jumped on my bike as the pedals started to roll...
The road to ourselves, and wind in hair,
The fresh air blowing away any care...
Nice cold creek dips to clear our bodies and soul,
Letting the clever water clear any mind control...
Feeling alive, we rode back home,
Then up our private creek we did roam...
The ancient forest holding us every step of the way,
Feeling so much gratitude for this every day...
Blessings from every tree,
I thank them for supporting me...

Loving Creativity

Creativity is life force in full flow,
The energy knows where it's to go...
Expanding consciousness through our creations,
It ripples out in many directions...
So trust what you're being guided to make,
And know that a certain state of presence it will take...
That presence as you create is such a gift,
And through your creations, humanity's vibration will lift...
So do, and create, and be in a loving state,
And the greatest gift, will be what you create...
So create, create, create,
When feeling inspired, do not wait...

Birth & Being

A new chapter of birth and being,
Releasing the mind control in the unseen...
Stories appearing out of the blue,
You're having to ask, are these true...
Or are they just memories from the past,
Trying to hold on, but they cannot last...
So release them and let them go,
So you can drop back into flow...

{ 180 }

Those That Align

How can I best support humanity at this time,
It's by sharing my teachings to those that align...
Creating my next book for those to see,
That the wisdom lives within them and me...
And if I can guide them back to the heart,
That is when their true blessings will start...
And they can share their teachings too,
All helping each other to find what's true...
I'm open for guidance on my next book,
And I'm grateful for the experience it took...
I'm being told as I start typing it up,
Life will start overflowing my energy cup...
It will be a stream of divinity,
And will unlock my creativity...

{ 181 }

Sacred Heart

It is not something that comes when someone says, 'I love you',
Because it's only in your heart that you'll feel what is true...
It doesn't come from someone else,
It can only be found within the self...
Many were taught that you must seek the love from another,
But it's unconditional, like your Earth Mother...
To seek would be to come from lack,
Then that is what you will attract...
When you find your divine connection, which has been with you all along,
You'll realise most of what you were taught, was actually wrong...
Your practice is to now stay in your heart,
That was your mission you were given from the start...

Weeding The Old

As she tends to the garden, bare feet & hands in the ground,
She realises there is a new passion she has found...
Pulling out the weeds keeps her present,
So any mind stories stay absent...
She sees the beauty in every little weed,
And with each one she pulls out, she plants a seed...
Seeding new thoughts as the old no longer take hold,
Seeing the lesson, they all had to unfold...
They at times can take over, if you don't take time to be still,
Any space in your mind, the weeds will fill...
So tend to your gardening each day,
And you'll be filled with blessings in a new way...

{ 183 }

Rainforest Bliss

The mountains holding us from every direction,
The creek providing us love and affection...
Rocks getting bigger the more we ventured up the track,
Swimming holes full of beauty, there was no lack...
My jaw dropping with awe at every turn,
But this beauty you did not have to earn...
You did not have to pay a fee or a ridiculous price,
Being able to enjoy your reflection was so nice...
The most ancient rainforest there is,
Being in the centre of it was pure bliss...
No one else to be seen,
We just soaked it up feeling so serene...
Plunge pools, water slides, rapids and waterfalls,
Rocks to climb and jump and also four legged crawls...
Laughter and joy radiating from my entire being,
I was so extremely grateful for what I was seeing...
I honoured the spirit of the land and all those that paved the way,
I am so blessed to get to experience Heaven on Earth each day...

{ 184 }

Who Am I

"Who am I", you may ask,
Finding the truth, is your task...
However, you won't find the truth outside yourself,
The guidance is to journey within the self...
You may wonder how that is done,
Letting go of external labels and things is where I began...
You are not your name, or your body, or your profession,
That may be the most challenging confession...
Because the ego mind likes to hold on,
And it will try telling you, I am wrong...
But I am the truth that lives within us all,
Give it a try, find stillness, it is your call...
Once you touch the truth, you'll understand,
Until then, none of this truth will actually land...

To Give Is The Gift

To give is to receive they say,
But it is a balancing act each day...
As sometimes you'll be the one with an over flowing cup,
So you'll be giving, to top another's energy up...
And other days it will be you who gets to receive,
All that good karma you'll get to retrieve...
An equal exchange takes place when you live from your heart,
And life will help you share your greatest art...
Whether its massage, cooking, cleaning, giving advice or something else,
All that genuine giving will come back to yourselves...
Life works in magical ways,
You'll be feeling blessed for the rest of your days...

Back To The Core

What wants to come through,
Is it a message for me or you...
Can you open your heart to feel your divine self,
Or are you still trying to seek it from someone else...
Drop from your mind to your heart,
That is where true oneness can start...
Feel the love as an energy of bliss within,
Practice on stopping any thoughts is where to begin...
Don't judge when the thoughts come,
Just observe them knowing they're done...
Eventually the mind will get more still,
And you'll be able to feel peace at your own will...
Once you can reach that stillness inside,
So much wisdom and guidance you will find...
But you won't have to search to find it,
As you'll just receive the knowing as you sit...
Enjoy your journey back to the core,
Trust your path, there is always more...

Secret To Living

I'll let you in on the greatest secret that's been kept from you,
This life as you know it is a lie and not true...
Your bodies don't actually exist,
Our ego minds we have to resist...
This is a human experience we are journeying through,
Nothing you've been taught was ever true...
You're creating your reality with your thoughts and belief,
So is there something you look at in disbelief...
If so, please know you've created this,
And you can also create more bliss...
You're more powerful than you may know,
You can create your Heaven on Earth, give it a go...
By focusing on the good things in your reality,
You'll start seeing evidence of your ability...
Once you see the true illusion of this cosmic life we are living,
You'll be more creative with the energy you're giving...
Life becomes a beautiful work of art,
And you can't help but live from your heart...
You see and feel the love creating your beautiful Heaven on Earth,
Realising that it's up to you what type of reality you birth...
I'm grateful you found yourself reading this,
And I'm excited for you to experience more bliss...

Peace In The Heart

There are so many distractions in every direction,
But you choose what gets your attention...
Your energy flows where your attention goes,
So be careful going where the ego flows...
It will try pull you under into the rough sea,
But your heart decides if that's where you want to be...
You may have allowed your ego free rein in the past,
And now you know you don't want that to last...
So now when you feel the ego creeping in,
You connect back to your heart within...
There is peace in the heart,
So that is where I like to start...

Waking Up To The Illusion

Are you living fully in the illusion,
If so, it will create much confusion...
Maybe you grew up watching TV,
Not realising the lies you would see...
You thought the news was real,
You'd even watch it while having a meal...
Ingesting all the stories filling you with fear,
Even being scared if a loved one came near...
You obeyed what the TV taught you,
Never even questioning what was true...
Now you start to realise you've lived a lie,
It would probably be hard not to break down and cry...
So allow the tears to release and let go,
Once you know the truth, you can live in full flow...
Unlearning everything that isn't from the heart,
Being gentle with yourself is the place to start...
We are all remembering at different stages,
So be kind to self as you journey through these pages...

Stop And Be

Her intuition is what starts her ignition guiding her where to go,
That is how she lives her life in full flow...
She is always amazed at what transpires when she trusts herself,
When she isn't distracted by everything else...
She spent less and less time on her phone,
And to the most magical places she continued to roam...
She used to always share the places she was guided to,
But then something else started to feel more true...
She was more present with the land and what she was seeing...
Time without her phone became so very freeing...
Seeing animals she had never seen or heard of before,
Her love for life became more and more...
Life being the presence that lives in all of us,
But connecting to your heart is a must...
Letting go of what the mind thinks you have to do,
Less thinking and you'll feel what is true...
It's not a truth that can be explained by the mind,
If you search for it, you will not find...
But if you spend more time in nature you will see,
The most beautiful reflection when you just stop and be...

{ 191 }

Water The Flowers

In your natural state you are divine,
Your inner light is here to shine...
But to shine in a way you may not know,
It's not a shining where everything is on show...
It's a deep journey in clearing the jungle of your mind,
Once you face your fears, many gifts you will find...
There may be snakes leading you astray,
Or maybe they make you run the other way...
There may be vines obscuring your track,
Which may divert you to go back...
Back to the past where that vine was just a small weed,
Maybe there is something your inner child may need...
Your attention and love maybe just the right seed,
So whatever has this vine tangled can be freed...
And then the pathway of your mind is clear,
And you've let go of that unnecessary fear...
The flowers of your mind no longer get you with their thorn,
Because there is so much of you that has been reborn...
Now the only thing to do,
Is water the flowers with what feels true...

Taking Flight

In nature I got shown things many don't see,
I saw how the animals live so free...
The sunbirds creating a hanging nest,
And there wasn't money they had to invest...
They gathered sticks and webs and paper bark from the trees,
And they weaved their nest with such ease...
Packing and prodding and making a nest called home,
Out into the forest they would roam...
Getting the nest ready to lay the eggs,
She'd climb in and wiggle down with her legs...
Once she had laid her eggs, she'd keep them warm,
She'd watch over them until they were born...
Once the eggs hatched, she gifted me the shell,
A gift of exchange as I said 'I'll watch over them well'...
And I stayed true to my word,
I'd stay close if it was danger, I heard...
She'd fly in to feed the chicks as they grew,
Such a beautiful process, I never knew...
Today I witnessed the little one take flight,
When the Mum came to feed them, they weren't in sight...
They had gained the courage to spread their wings,
Now I'm sure they're feeling the freedom it brings...

{ 193 }

Demons Of The Mind

Demons only exist in the mind,
When in your heart, you will not find...
Our mind is the so-called devil they speak about,
It's that ego voice in your head that will sometimes shout...
It's fighting to save its home,
Through lots of fears it likes to roam...
Bringing the debris to mess with your peace,
But if in your heart all you will feel is ease...
So if ever you're wondering if you're in your heart or head,
If its not peace you feel then it's the ego mind you have fed...
Don't allow the ego to take control,
Or more stories will quickly unroll...
And before you know it, you'll be swamped with negativity,
Instead, be in your heart, open to divine receptivity...

Compassion Lives In The Heart

Compassion is a recognition that lives within us all,
And for it to come forth requires the ego to fall...
If we can't have compassion for someone else,
Ask, 'where don't we have that compassion for the self'...
Life is always providing us with ways to evolve and grow,
And will illuminate areas for growth that maybe we didn't know...
It can be hard at first to find compassion for some,
Maybe we feel they don't deserve it for what they have done...
This only prevents us from coming home to oneness,
And also leaves humanity in a state of separated mess...
So remember to come back to the heart,
That is where the compassion will start...

Greed And Wealth

I woke with this poem that wanted to come through,
Maybe there is a message in there for you...
I know it's getting more expensive to live,
But is that what makes you not want to give...
When we're trying to break free from a world of greed & wealth,
Which is run by people that don't care about your health...
We have to also look within ourselves,
And see what we are expecting from everyone else...
Are you asking a ridiculous price for an hour call,
If so, maybe it's from your ego you need to fall...
Back into your heart to have a conversation,
Not expecting a large compensation...
It saddens me so much to see,
And I experienced it through me...
Being left not able to pay rent,
My mental health sure got a dent...
But it showed me there has to be another way,
Where we all support each other each day...
The ego self may need to die,
And it may even ask why...
Because the ego is fueled by greed and wealth,
And will mess with your mental health...

Divinely Aligned

I know it can be expensive to live,
But it sure does feel good to give...
And when you give without expecting anything back,
The law of attraction will make sure you're never in lack...

Question Within

Our pain bodies are our ego mind,
In it there is no peace to find...
But if you observe it you will see,
When staying present you'll become so free...
Freeing yourself from the ego that wants control,
If you allow it attention, then it will take its toll...
It will have you acting out past stories from another time,
To other pain bodies you will also align...
Which ego will win the fight,
No consciousness can be in sight...
Because anytime there is separation in your life,
Question within if you need to think twice...
Not allowing the ego to take you from your heart,
It is a beautiful journey which inspired this poetic art...

Releasing Addiction

What is addiction in the current day,
It's something that has control and the final say...
It comes in many a different form,
And it will become somewhat of your norm...
It will drag you under like a huge wave,
And it will be something that you crave...
It could be smoking, drinking, drugs or sex,
Or maybe you're addicted to your phone and text...
Maybe it's a habit that you can't give up,
Maybe it's a 'healthy addiction' that fills your cup...
But any addiction is relying on something outside yourself,
You're unconsciously seeking to fill a need from something else...
Maybe you've been able to quit that thing you've craved each day,
And now another addiction has come your way...
Addiction is easily replaced with another distraction,
You'll keep swapping addictions until you find inner satisfaction...
You can't weed out addiction by using any outside tool,
You'll need to find the root and use your strength to pull...
Releasing the root from the core,
So it has no hold on you any more...

Vibration Is A Choice

We have the ability to control our internal vibration,
We've had this gift since the start of creation...
However, it does come down to personal choice,
If we decide to listen to the ego voice...
The ego will thrive on keeping your vibration low,
So I'll share with you what I've learnt and know...
If you spend more time focusing on the silver lining,
More blessings you will then be aligning...
But if you constantly focus on what's wrong,
In a lower vibration you will belong...
It's like strengthening the mind at your inner gym,
Strength and determination will have you win...
Don't be discouraged if you fall off the track,
With that simple awareness you will attract...
Many more blessing that come your way,
There will be synchronicities every day...
Showing you have raised your vibration,
And life will be constant celebration...

Present Gift

If you're always living in the future thinking ahead,
Or if you're stuck in the past with old memories in your head...
You're missing the gifts of this moment here,
It is the present that will bring a gratitude filled tear...
So this year at Christmas may you know,
That your presence can be with you everywhere you go...
It is the gift that will keep giving,
And when you give it, you'll truly be living...

Sea Change

If ever you find yourself feeling blue,
I've got a suggestion that may help you…
Get outside and head to the beach,
If you're lucky you may see a whale breach…
The energy from being by the salty sea,
Will have you feeling so light and free…
It cleanses away what serves you no more,
Going to the beach where there's so much to adore…
The refreshing water nourishing the soul,
A letting go of any sort of control…
Just flowing and drifting and admiring the view,
If only you knew going to the beach was all you had to do…
But now you'll know what you need,
For any stagnant energy to be freed…

{ 201 }

Planting The Seeds

Seeding is a time of manifesting,
Being intentional with what you're creating...
Maybe its beautiful flowers you want to see,
And maybe its just more spare time to be...
Maybe there is something you are being called to birth,
Which will assist humanity in this time of rebirth...
Maybe there is something else you're calling in,
It's now time to set your intentions from within...
So when the time is right your seed will flower for all to see,
You'll radiate delight as you took this time to just be...

{ 202 }

Treasure Map

With her eagle vision she sees it all,
And not just because she stands tall...
Sometimes she sees more than the eyes can see,
It's what happens when she stops to be...
Visions pop into her mind,
A puzzle not many find...
But maybe they have their own puzzle to find,
By staying true to themself, their pieces they will find...
The pieces may be more like a treasure map,
The more you piece it together, the more you'll attract...
It's a fun game, this one known as life,
Staying true to you, will keep you out of strife...

Connect To The Heart

To become magnetic to all I desire,
It's through my hand that I will inspire...
Through writing, dancing, massage or art,
Because my hand is connected to my heart...
It heals and channels and acts as a gateway,
Not listening to what the ego mind may say...
Because it's connected to the oneness of all beings,
And works so effortlessly as it seems...
But when present, the mind isn't in the way,
So there are no ego thoughts at play...
Just bliss for me and the energy running through me,
I help others reach that place within, so easily...
Where they remember they're able to connect to their eternal self,
They don't need to rely on the help from somebody else...
I just point them in the right direction,
So they can feel their inner connection...

{ 204 }

Presence Of Love

How can I best serve humanity,
Is it by me releasing more of my poetry...
Or is it in person connection,
So I can steer them in the right direction...
Maybe just my presence is enough,
By holding the frequency of love...
Maybe that is all that is needed,
The highest intentions have been seeded...
What I came here to do,
Is to stay in alignment with what's true...

… { 205 }

What Are You Creating

We are the ones programming ourselves,
So we must stop blaming anything else...
As that only gives our power away,
And is the devil's work at play...
The devil can also be known as the ego mind,
If you feed it, then more drama you will find...
Focusing on a force outside of yourself,
Is giving your energy away to something else...
And we are here to evolve and grow,
That is what I deep down know...
Where your attention goes,
The energy will surely flow...
So if you keep feeding the so-called beast,
Of your energy field it will continue to feast...
So the advice that is coming through,
Is to connect to your heart to know what is true...
In every moment you're helping to create a heaven or hell,
So ask yourself where you want to dwell...
The choice is love or fear,
Choose one and the other will disappear...

{ 206 }

Divinely Aligned Timing

I let go of work and surrendered any plan,
And then I was guided to a divine man...
A connection I'd yearned for, for so long,
But I had to find where I did belong...
I'd travelled to countries far and wide,
And had even journeyed deep inside...
Finding pieces of the puzzle along the way,
Because I was following what the whispers would say...
A soul map guiding me home to my eternal self,
Where I wasn't searching for anyone else...
Connected to my heart, I was connected to all,
So in love we did not have to fall...
As we had both found the love within,
The most beautiful reflection we did bring...
It was such divine timing when and where we met,
A day of synchronicities I'll never forget...
For many years I'd heard 'meet at the tree',
And now I realise it was the Daintree...
A moment sooner, we wouldn't have aligned,
As it was perfectly orchestrated, and divinely timed...

Switch Off

I've been quiet online for a while now,
The places I've been exploring are just 'wow'...
I observed the part of me that loves to share these places,
And decided I'd be more present & connected with these spaces...
It was really hard at first,
Wanting to reach for my phone was a real thirst...
I realised it had become somewhat of an attachment to me,
Me without my phone was a rare sight to see...
But I didn't want to lose myself in my phone,
I wanted to enjoy where I was being guided to roam...
So I stopped carrying my phone with me as I explored,
And I saw so much more that I adored...
I made connections with those who weren't lost in their device,
Enjoying each other's company in person was so nice...
It's amazing to see what happens when you mix things up,
You'll find more natural ways of being that fill your cup...
So I invite you to give it a go,
Leave your phone at home and be in full flow...

… 208 …

The First Breath

Our life begins with the first breath we take,
We entered this planet where we chose to awake…
But awake to what you may ask,
That is your human experience task…
As you grow and learn and adapt,
You'll start seeing certain things you attract…
They may not be things you deep down desire,
So you realise some beliefs you may need to rewire…
You may need to unlearn the things you were taught to believe,
The more unlearning you do, the more gifts you receive…
The gifts being a remembrance of who you were before the first breath was taken,
This can be a big realisation and may have you shaken…
But deep within your core,
You always knew there was so much more…
So if the first breath is what got you here,
And the last breath is when you disappear…
All the answers can be found between the breaths we take,
So breathing consciously is a choice only you can make…
The simple tool you have access to at any time,
Is the gift that will help you access the divine…
The divine being the connection to all that is,

Divinely Aligned

It's accessed through the heart and is pure bliss...
So breath into your heart and you will see,
You're a gift of love here to help awaken humanity...

Prioritise Rest

Make sure you prioritise enough rest,
It is the key ingredient for being at your best...
In this day and age we can get so busy with so many things to do,
But you need to question, is it really serving you...
Because if you don't slow down and include rest in your day,
Life will eventually force you to stop in another way...
It may not be of your choosing, but you'll eventually see,
That what is needed is to come back to a life of simplicity...
So how can you add more rest in your day-to-day life,
It may not seem productive, but it will keep you out of strife...
And you'll actually get a lot more done,
When the fear of not doing enough, you overcome...

How To Handle Grief

Firstly, let's figure out what grief is,
Is it a feeling about something you miss...
Is grief a sadness for what you've had to let go,
Or is it a feeling of love that is deeper than you know...
A feeling of home reflected by another,
Maybe it was a friend or your father or mother...
Either way those feelings can take us under,
And they sure do make me wonder...
If the grief is actually because of the love that was felt,
Then it's the greatest gift that we have been dealt...
As they reflected a love to us that is true,
They were the reflection of what's in you...
So the love is carried around in your heart forever,
So when you're feeling down, tune into your heart and it's them you'll remember...
So even if you can no longer see them, they are always there,
Reminding you through your heart of the love you'll always share...

Dream Meaning

Have you ever woken up from a dream,
And wondered, what does that even mean...
Are dreams real or are they fake,
When we are dreaming are we actually awake...
The mind may not be able to comprehend,
For all the possibilities there is no end...
There are dreams that illuminate our fear,
But its ultimately our choice what comes near...
Your dreams may also show you your desire,
So do you let your dreams truly inspire...
Do you take action on what you're to do,
Your dreams may hold the ultimate clue...
Maybe you don't remember your dreams when you wake,
And maybe there are some you just want to shake...
But our dreams can show us we are creating our own reality,
So if of your dreams you need more clarity...
You should get in contact with Dreamhub Mel,
She'll help you to realise what your dreams are trying to tell...

Confusion

Confusion can be a common thing,
And much sadness it can bring...
Wondering why things had to end,
Or how your heart will ever mend...
Maybe you've suddenly been let go of your job,
So of your purpose you feel you've been robbed...
It may not make sense to the mind,
And the answer you'll probably never find...
But if you surrender and let go,
You'll be able to drop into full flow...
Life is guiding you somewhere new,
And there is nothing you need to do...
Except keep staying true to you,
And doors will open out of the blue...
You'll look back on this time,
And see how it was all so divine...
You're supported more than you know,
And soon all that support will show...
So relax and enjoy the power of now,
And magical blessings will come to you somehow...

{ 213 }

Healing Journey

When someone is on their healing journey, what do they mean,
They may be uncovering the illusions from their old way of being...
This can be a big process as they slowly uncover,
All their inner gifts they were yet to discover...
As the layers start peeling,
They find more gifts revealing...
It may not be a linear path,
But trusting the process becomes their task...
As they don't yet know what they don't know,
And there are many paths they can choose to go...
Each path is perfectly guiding them back to their heart,
They realise that was the actual mission from the start...
There is no actual map for this journey,
But you'll find puzzle pieces as you realise you're worthy...
No two people have the exact same puzzle to piece together,
But they may hold puzzle pieces for each other...
So when you trust where you are being guided to go,
More of your puzzle pieces will then show...
When you piece the puzzle pieces together you will see,
The healing journey is what will set you free...
A remembrance of all you hold within,
Then your life can truly begin...

… }

Waking Up to A New Day

You know those days you feel you've gotten out of the wrong side of the bed,
No matter what you do, the frustrations keep running around in your head…
Those days where nothing seems to go right,
And there seems no end to it in sight…
Well this poem is about those days,
And things that may help in so many ways…
How you start your day is such an important thing,
Because it dictates the energy that you bring…
And what you give is what you get,
So you want to keep any sneaky thoughts in check…
Firstly, how do you wake up each day,
Is it by a horrible beeping alarm that starts to play…
Giving you anxiety for your day ahead,
All before you even got out of bed…
Or do you start your day listening to the news and what they say,
Which just creates and adds more fear and anxiety to your day…
Or do you choose to make the day yours and flow with ease,
Maybe that means starting it outside in the fresh breeze…
Moving your body the way that feels good to you,
Then your body will treat you the same way too…

RACHEL HEANEY

Maybe you like to tune into your breath and still your mind,
Then there will be more gratitude to find...
And when you notice the blessings in this moment in time,
To more blessing you will easily align...
You'll flow so easily through your day,
Because you started your day in a better way...

… { 215 }

Love, In Full Flow

Love, in full flow is what I was calling in,
And of course, that is what life did bring…
I'd given up my search for finding love from another,
Because I'd realised, I am my own internal lover…
So I was living my life in full flow,
Trusting where I was guided to go…
No distractions or plans on where I was to be,
I just had the subtle whispers that were guiding me…
So I followed them before the mind got in the way,
And then the most beautiful alignment happened one day…
I was guided to the most divine man,
And instantly, I was his greatest fan…
Because he was a divine reflection of me,
And when I stopped searching outside, it was him I got to see…
It's the irony of living in full flow,
There's so much you'll need to let go…
But life had a plan I couldn't yet see,
I just followed the whispers to meet at the tree…

{ 216 }

Blessings From Above

Have you ever experienced a blissful feeling like never before,
A stillness from slowing down and tuning into your core...
This is a glimmer of your natural state of being,
When you stop and be it is so very freeing...
Then more blessings come your way with ease and grace,
When you are present there is no challenge to face...
Because you become a channel of pure love,
Where more blessings are sent from above...
So keep finding that stillness within,
And enjoy the feeling of love it will bring...

{ 217 }

Down To Earth

When someone is 'down to Earth', what does that even mean,
Does it mean that on Earth, there's lots of places they've been...
Or does it mean they connect to the Earth with their bare feet,
Or is it all the Earth's inhabitants that they're happy to greet...
Or maybe they are grounded in their body, not just their mind,
So there's a sense of peace around them, that you will find...
Maybe they birth the new down to this Earth,
Maybe they've realised they're a pillar through this rebirth...
Maybe they've found the truth deep within,
So it is a sense of stability and oneness they bring...

Decluttering The Mind

Decluttering can bring such a beautiful gift,
And it will eventually help your energy uplift...
Because if you're caged in with so much stuff,
The space you search for will never be enough...
As the peace is found in the emptiness of your mind,
If in your external reality there is no peace you find...
You must declutter and let go of the things keeping you stuck,
Be ruthless with letting go, just throw it in the truck...
Take it to the tip or better still,
Donate things to others from your own free will...
Because when we give, it clears more space for us,
And having a clear head space, is a must...
You'll feel such a relief when it's done,
Being in the process doesn't always feel fun...
But the more things that you let go,
The more you'll be able to live in full flow...
You'll feel so alive when the decluttering is done,
It will feel like it's the lottery you've just won...

Christmas In the Eyes of a Child

Christmas is coming, it's almost here,
I feel the excitement because Santa is near...
I wonder what list I'm on,
Is it the naughty or nice one I belong...
I better make sure I'm extra nice to Mum and Dad,
Because Santa will know if I've been bad...
And I don't want to end up with a piece of coal,
Because getting lots of presents is my goal...
I'll ask Santa for all I've been wishing for,
And if I'm good, he'll deliver them, and so much more...
I'll leave the reindeers and Santa carrots and beer,
And if I hear them in the night, I'll have nothing to fear...
I'll stay in my bed resting my head,
I have to wait for morning until I can get out of bed...
I'll rush to see what's under the tree,
Wondering what Santa left for me...
I will then wake up Mum and Dad to show them too,
They will feel my excitement hit them out of the blue...
The fun and excitement has only just begun,
Because we're going to Nay Nay & Paddy's house for more fun...

RACHEL HEANEY

We'll get to see the family and celebrate together,
And create more fun memories that will last forever...

{ 220 }

Love Is Our Savior

When you realise no one is coming to save you, it's up to you,
Finding the path back to your heart is what you have to do...
It can be the simplest and hardest task at the same time,
But when in your heart, it's when you'll truly align...
For humanity as a whole to survive,
We need to find the truth of being alive...
And we can't know that truth in our mind,
Drop into your heart and the answers you'll find...
The only thing that can save us is the love in our heart,
And it's also where you'll create the greatest art...
Allowing others a map pointing the way,
But it's up to the love in our hearts each day...
So connect there as you focus on the love,
Simply being connected to your heart is enough...

{ 221 }

State Of Lust

When you're in a state of lust,
It's your mind that thinks it's a must...
You've attached an idea in your mind about the object of your attention,
Being in lust will never help you on your path of ascension...
Lust is simply a construct of your mind,
No peace in it you will ever find...
And if you get what you're lusting for,
You'll realise you just want more...
Searching for something outside of you,
Creates a path of destruction, it's true...
Once you realise that lust is just a distraction set up by the ego self,
You'll remember that no freedom can come from anyone else...
So each time you notice lust arise,
Know it's the ego in disguise...
And come back to the wholeness in your heart,
Where no egoic desires can even start...

{ 222 }

Sliding Door Moments

Have you ever wondered about how your life can change in the blink of an eye,
Where you felt to go somewhere, but didn't, later wondering why...
In every moment there are different sliding door moments that we face,
When we open one door, we could be sent to another place...
A place where there are more things to adore,
But what if you'd chosen to ignore a certain door...
So the lessons of life keep coming your way,
But you'll get an opportunity of that door again one day...
The doors are all like a maze leading to the centre,
Because of free will we get to choose which ones we enter...
Maybe we like a maze full of trials and tribulations,
Or maybe we like a maze where we birth lots of creations...
Maybe we want to journey through the maze with certain others,
Maybe we want to experience being Mothers...
Maybe we like to find hidden doors to explore,
Where we find access to so much more...
No matter what, every door we choose is perfect for us,
It's what our soul's chosen, so trusting is a must...
Knowing that every door leads you eventually to the same place,
It's about the journey we take and experiences we face...

RACHEL HEANEY

Always getting clearer on what door we want to open next,
And hopefully this poem has given you more context...

{ 223 }

False Light

As you open within to more light,
There will be more darkness in your sight...
You may not be able to see it with your eyes,
It may sneak up on you and be in disguise...
It may be dressed up trying to deceive you,
So you need to be discerning with what is true...
There is a lot of darkness masked behind false light,
It's actually just their ego that wants to shine bright...
They may also try to make you feel you need what they're selling,
Be aware and discerning if it's the heart or ego they're dwelling...
Do they genuinely want to support you to evolve and grow,
Or are they actually guiding you away from living in flow...
Trusting yourself is the greatest gift you'll ever own,
Through false light ceremonies you'll not have to roam...
So keep coming back to the truth in your heart,
The mind control will try to enter but don't let it start...
Heart based living is the key and needed at this time,
Then, to other heart-based people, you will align...
Not just people that are needing your energy to fuel their ego,
That old way of business and leadership needs to go...
Come back to your heart and you will see,
That false light ceremonies are not where you need to be...

{ 224 }

Twists & Turns

Life will present you with many twists and turns,
And there will be much you may have to unlearn...
This human experience will help you evolve to a new level of being,
There has been so much that's been hiding in the unseen...
The lights being shone onto the darkness, to expose the truth that's been hidden,
I trust you've felt the truth as journeying through this book, and the words that were written...
Remember to connect to your heart each day,
And you will be able to feel the truth in every way...

Acknowledgement

Thank you to all those who purchased this book,
Or who took the time to have a look...
Also to those that have reached out to me,
Because my poems have helped them break free...

Thank you to all my loved ones who had patience with me,
As I took time out to release this book for all to see...

Thanks to all who suggested poem ideas for me to write,
I was always amazed with what appeared in my sight...
I'm so grateful I get to share them in this way,
Supporting others with the inspired poems each day...

A big thanks to my friend Hannah Dennis,
For capturing the front and back cover of this...
If you also want some photos in full flow,
You can find Hannah's details just below...
www.hannah-dennis.com

If you have any suggestions of what I write next,
Stay in contact below or send me a text...

Instagram: @rach_heaney

Acknowledgement

www.ingramcontent.com/pod-product-compliance
Lightning Source LLC
Chambersburg PA
CBHW051423290426
44109CB00016B/1410